Creating an Innovative Culture

Dennis Sherwood

T0341420

- ■ Fast track route to making innovation happen

- ■ Covers the key ingredients of cultures that actively stimulate and encourage innovation, from idea generation and evaluation to the five key motivators and the five key enablers that ensure that great ideas come to fruition

- ■ Examples and lessons from some of the world's most creative businesses, including Goldman Sachs and 3M, and ideas from the smartest thinkers, including James Christiansen and Edward de Bono

- ■ Includes a glossary of key concepts and a comprehensive resources guide

≫EXPRESS EXEC.COM≪
essential management thinking at your fingertips

First published 2002 by
Capstone Publishing (a Wiley company)
8 Newtec Place
Magdalen Road
Oxford OX4 1RE
United Kingdom
http://www.capstoneideas.com

CIP catalogue records for this book are available from the British Library and the US Library of Congress

ISBN 1-84112-386-2

Printed and bound in Great Britain

This book is printed on acid-free paper

Contents

Introduction to ExpressExec

ExpressExec is 3 million words of the latest management thinking compiled into 10 modules. Each module contains 10 individual titles forming a comprehensive resource of current business practice written by leading practitioners in their field. From brand management to balanced scorecard, ExpressExec enables you to grasp the key concepts behind each subject and implement the theory immediately. Each of the 100 titles is available in print and electronic formats.

Through the ExpressExec.com Website you will discover that you can access the complete resource in a number of ways:

» printed books or e-books;
» e-content – PDF or XML (for licensed syndication) adding value to an intranet or Internet site;
» a corporate e-learning/knowledge management solution providing a cost-effective platform for developing skills and sharing knowledge within an organization;
» bespoke delivery – tailored solutions to solve your need.

Why not visit www.expressexec.com and register for free key management briefings, a monthly newsletter and interactive skills checklists. Share your ideas about ExpressExec and your thoughts about business today.

Please contact elound@wiley-capstone.co.uk for more information.

Introduction to Creating an Innovative Culture

This chapter sets the scene by describing why organizational culture is critical in allowing innovation to flourish . . . or in killing it stone dead.

WHY CULTURE IS SO IMPORTANT FOR INNOVATION

As I describe in the accompanying title *Innovation Express*, innovation isn't simply having a great idea: in the business world, innovation is about managing a four-stage process:

1 **idea generation** – in which the initial ideas are created;
2 **evaluation** – in which a decision is taken as to which ideas to progress, and which to discard, at least for the present;
3 **development** – in which an idea is made fully fit-for-purpose;
4 **implementation** – in which the idea is brought to full fruition.

Furthermore, innovation isn't just about developing new products; the need for new ideas, and to make something happen with those ideas, applies to all these domains too:

» **processes** – as exemplified by the best examples of business process reengineering;
» **structures** – in terms of new forms of organization;
» **relationships** – for example, new forms of external relationships with customers or suppliers, or new forms of internal relationships within your own organization;
» **strategy** – in the form not only of new innovative strategies, but also as regards the process of strategy formulation;
» **you!** – for maybe the most fundamental form of innovation is the acceptance, within my mind – or indeed your mind – that maybe there really is a better idea out there!

These can all be represented on the **Innovation Target** (Fig. 1.1)

Yes, innovation is much, much more than having bright ideas. And although idea generation is an activity that can be carried out by individuals, or ideally by small groups (see, for example, Chapter 6 of *Innovation Express*), the other activities – evaluation, development, and implementation – require organizational cooperation and coordination. No single individual has all the skills, let alone the resources, to take an idea right through to implementation, and even small groups can find this very difficult – that's why so many businesses, started by an inventor, or a small team of enthusiasts, fail.

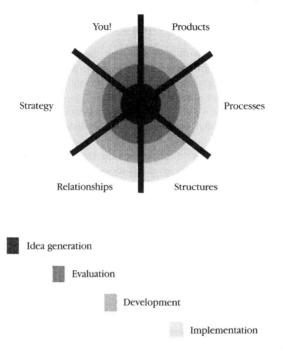

You! Products

Strategy Processes

Relationships Structures

■ Idea generation

■ Evaluation

■ Development

Implementation

Fig. 1.1

And because the processes of evaluation, development, and implementation depend on organizational cooperation and coordination, making innovation happen depends on how well people within the organization cooperate with one another, and how well the organization itself coordinates resources. These, of course, are all aspects of interpersonal behavior, of management style, of culture. An organization's success – or otherwise – in making innovation happen is therefore totally dependent on its culture.

And that's what this title is all about:

» to explore all those aspects of organizational culture that are particularly relevant to innovation;

» to describe what *you* can do to build a culture that encourages, supports, and delivers innovation in all its richness.

Organizations that can do this also reap the reward – the reward of being able to solve problems, to grasp opportunities, to create their own future. The organizational capability to innovate truly confers the ultimate competitive advantage.

This title will therefore focus on those aspects of innovation which require organizational cooperation and coordination – namely, the three stages of evaluation, development, and implementation. For completeness, the following box summarizes the key points of the first stage of idea generation: much more information is to be found in the accompanying title *Innovation Express*, and the whole field of innovation is explored in depth in my book *Smart Things to Know about Innovation and Creativity*, published by Capstone in 2001.

IDEA GENERATION – THE KEY PRINCIPLES

» **Koestler's Law** states that creativity – the generation of new ideas – is not a matter of luck or genius. Rather, it can be made to happen by a deliberate process of searching for new patterns of existing components.

» For innovation in business, the components that need to be recombined to form the new patterns are not laid bare, like the notes on a piano. Rather, they exist bundled together in existing patterns – the patterns of our knowledge, learning, and experience.

» As a consequence, before a new pattern can be formed, the old patterns need to be broken apart – only then can the component parts be uncovered, and made available for new pattern formation.

» This process of breaking apart our knowledge, learning, and experience is one of **unlearning**. Most people find unlearning very difficult to do, especially when we have been successful.

» All the tools and techniques of creativity are mechanisms to help you unlearn. In general, these tools fall into two categories – **springboards** and **retro-fits**.

» Springboards are processes that take as the starting point your existing knowledge, learning, and experience. The *InnovAction!* process, for example, takes this, identifies the underlying elements, and uses the question "How might this be different?" to discover new ideas (see Chapter 6 of *Innovation Express*).

» Retro-fits, such as the random word technique, project your imagination into a different domain, and encourage you to discover new ideas by retro-fitting from the different domain back to the focus of attention.

So, after that lightning-fast review of everything-you-need-to-know-about-idea-generation, let's start by taking a closer look at the second stage of the Innovation Target, the process of evaluation . . .

What Do We Mean by Evaluation?

This chapter examines "evaluation" - the organizational process by which ideas get judged as "good" or "bad" - and shows firstly, why it is central to innovation in general, and secondly, why the organizational culture is so important as regards how evaluation takes place.

HOW DOES EVALUATION WORK IN YOUR ORGANIZATION?

Evaluation – the second zone from the center of the Innovation Target – is the process by which ideas are selected for further development, or, alternatively, rejected. Stated as simply as that, evaluation sounds as if it's a well-ordered and effective process that every business does in a professional way as a matter of course.

EVALUATION IN ACTION

As a result of a recent review of overhead expenditure, a study team has identified that your organization's recruitment process for middle managers (in the age bracket 30–35) is cumbersome (there are many interviews before a candidate can be given an offer), time-consuming (the process can extend over three months), and expensive (in terms of interviewer time, assessment centers, and candidates' expenses). This is causing a number of good candidates to withdraw before an offer is made, and there is also some disappointment with the quality of those candidates who do join, but don't seem to come up to expectations after a year in the organization.

You are a departmental manager attending a meeting to discuss this, and since you are not directly involved with recruitment, you have no particular axe to grind – your key objective is to help contribute to the discussion of ideas as to how to improve the recruitment process.

During the meeting, a junior manager, newly recruited herself, says: "What about this for an idea? Why don't we dispense with most of our process altogether, but offer three-month temporary contracts to candidates that have got particularly good CVs? If they work out, we can then make their contract permanent; if not, they can go."

What is your immediate reaction to this idea?

Most people's immediate reaction is "That's nuts." So, if that was your reaction too, you are not alone. And most people would have no angst about saying so in the meeting, either directly, or in terms of the umpteen reasons why that idea wouldn't work, such as:

» "As soon as word got out, we'd be flooded with crazy applicants."
» "We'd never be able to get rid of those that don't make the grade."
» "No good applicant would be willing to join on a three-month contract."
» "It's illegal."
» "We'd be taken to every employment tribunal under the sun."

I'm sure you can think of many more.

In all probability, after a few minutes, that idea will be dismissed as lunatic, and the meeting will move on to more "serious" suggestions. And, as a result, the junior manager will have learned a very important organizational lesson: to be very careful about when to open her mouth, and even more careful about what she ever dares to suggest. But that's not the only result. The organization has lost out too, for by dissuading someone from making a suggestion, the organization is losing the opportunity for someone else to build on the original suggestion, and take it further, perhaps to a very good idea indeed. As I describe in Chapter 6 of *Innovation Express*, an important part of the idea generation process is the way in which teams work together, with people springboarding off one another's contributions – a process that can work only if individuals are willing to make a contribution in the first place.

What is happening here, of course, is the process of evaluation – but few of us think of this natural, everyday business interaction in such formal terms. An idea has been tabled – that the organization might change its recruitment process in a very radical way – and as soon as the words are uttered, we immediately form a judgment as to whether the idea is "good" or "bad." What else is this but evaluation? And how do we make this judgment? Are we influenced by who made the suggestion? Are we influenced by whether or not we are potentially threatened by the suggestion? Or by whether we immediately like or dislike the idea? Or by whether or not we like the person who suggested the idea? Or whether or not we feel it is in our career interests to be seen to be supporting the idea, opposing it, or remaining detached?

My experience is that we are influenced by all of these things, and many more too. Our reaction to new ideas – especially radical ones – is a complex mixture of detached judgment and personal emotion, of business experience and organizational politics.

EVALUATION IN ACTION REVISITED

With reference to the last box, what would have been your own reaction, and the reaction of the meeting, had the same suggestion been put forward by:

» the company chairman?
» the company chief executive?
» the human resources director?
» the senior manager responsible for recruitment?
» the company lawyer?
» a recently recruited middle manager?
» a candidate?
» a secretary?

Mmm. Is evaluation in your organization ultimately a question of power? If it is, then this is very real, very human, very believable. But from a business point of view, the key question is "Is this wise?" Does it make good business sense for ideas to be evaluated in such a cavalier, off-hand, and political manner? And is it wise to build into the organizational culture all sorts of fears, all manner of subtle, unstated, pressures that result in only the most banal ideas ever being tabled?

My answer to all these questions – of course – is "No – that isn't wise at all!" But is there a way of conducting the process of idea evaluation in a more robust, more professional manner? A way that encourages people to continue to suggest ideas without feeling they are risking their careers, but one that still filters out the lulus, so we don't bet the company either? A way that clearly identifies the risks associated with the idea, enabling us to determine how those risks can be assessed and managed? Clearly, what we are seeking is a question of balance: a process that stimulates idea generation, but can still distinguish the pie-in-the-sky from the blockbuster; a process that avoids the worst of organizational politics, but rewards integrity and honesty; a process that passes the "due diligence" test that enables us to say with pride, even five years later, that the decision we took was the best possible, given the information we had at the time.

YES – A WISE PROCESS DOES EXIST!

The good news is that such a process does indeed exist, so let me highlight the key points here.

Firstly, we need to recognize that evaluation takes place in three different ways:

» Formally, in the context, for example, of business cases and project approvals. Each organization has its own way of doing these: typically, the process involves the review of written proposals by a panel that meets at defined intervals, say every three months, with the outcome that approved projects are funded, rejected projects are shelved, and any on which decisions can't be taken are sent back to their originators for further work.

» Informally, in small groups, in meetings and discussions. This is the process of largely unconscious, inadvertent, and unwitting, evaluation that takes place in all our group interactions – as the last two boxes illustrated. This is how more junior people learn what is right, wrong, accepted, unacceptable, dangerous, safe; this is how more senior people can exert subtle, and not-so-subtle, influence; this is a major mechanism whereby organizational cultures become defined, are made explicit, and are maintained.

» Personally, in our own heads. As a result of our experience with other people, we all learn what is safe to say, to whom, when. Our innermost censor plays a major role in determining what we choose to say, how we choose to say it, from whom we are most likely to receive the most favorable response, and just when the time is right to speak up or to stay silent. If this rings a bell with you, then perhaps it is this inner censor which is the most significant block to innovation in your organization; or, to express the same idea in a different way, what is it about your organizational culture that causes people to be so fearful of putting new ideas on the table?

In many organizations, the formal process of business cases and project approval is far too slow and ponderous, and, in its worst manifestation, can act as the ultimate block to organizational innovation: by the time an idea reaches the project panel, it has been sanitized and made safe, with all the radical – and the most innovative – elements long since excised. Sluggish, long-winded, and highly political processes, however, are not the only way of playing this game, and we shall see how to make this process far more effective in Chapters 6 and 7.

Much more important are the group and personal processes: aware managers, of course, know that these interact intimately, for the private, personal process is heavily conditioned by what happens in public, in groups. They know that a culture in which the informal group process acts as a disincentive on individuals creates a climate of fear and embarrassment, and so discourages people from doing anything other than grunt their reluctant agreement with their boss's ideas. Good managers know how to build a culture that strikes a wise balance between two apparently contradictory concepts: a culture which is supportive of the individual and of the individual's ideas, encouraging people to articulate ideas, however apparently half-baked, as well as one which is professional, rigorous, and fair, in which all ideas, when well thought through, are subject to careful scrutiny, so enabling the selection of the very best ideas to be progressed. I discuss how to go about building such a culture in the next several chapters, and how this can be helped by the use of a number of tools and techniques. One key concept, however, is this:

AVOID PREMATURE EVALUATION

Many people – especially dominant younger males – become over-excited when ideas are discussed. If it's their idea, they are incredibly enthusiastic, optimistic, persuasive; if it's someone else's idea, they are hypercritical, scathing, damning. This condition is known as "premature evaluation," and is very disappointing for all concerned.

Wise managers know that no ideas are born with a business case attached – they just aren't. And wise managers know that adversarial attacks such as "That's crazy, we don't stand a hope of making money out of that!", "We tried that before you joined the company and it was a total failure!", and "How much revenue do you think that will make, then?" aren't smart at all, they're just put-downs. So wise managers don't evaluate prematurely, and they help build internal processes in their organizations which allow time and space for ideas to be developed to a sufficient state of robustness that they can be evaluated fairly and professionally. That means that genuinely good ideas are backed, no matter who originated them; and when ideas are rejected, the originators are not damaged, but positively encouraged to come up with more and more new ideas.

Wise managers also know the importance of language and the power of phrases such as "Tell me more about that", "What do we have to do to make that work?", and "What resources do you need to work that idea up into a full business case?"

By building a culture which avoids premature evaluation, but one which is still rigorously professional, the good manager can gain the best of all possible worlds – an organization in which weak ideas are rejected without discouraging people from trying again, while the very best ideas are funded through to the next stages of development and implementation. I will discuss the cultural conditions for these in Chapters 6 and 7: the next chapter looks at evaluation as a business process in its own right.

Evaluation as a Business Process

This chapter explains why the process of evaluation needs to be transparent, complete, balanced, speedy, responsive, and pragmatic.

EVALUATION IS ALL ABOUT TAKING WISE DECISIONS

Once idea generation – such as the *InnovAction!* process described in Chapter 6 of *Innovation Express* – gets motoring, ideas get generated in their hundreds. A two-day idea generation workshop can easily produce three or four hundred new ideas, even if many members of the group have never used the *InnovAction!* method before. During the workshop, as the energy level rises, people write their ideas on brightly colored A5 index cards, which are then stuck on the wall, and, every now and again, the group clusters the cards together according to various themes. As participants read the cards, more ideas come to mind, and more cards go up.

Some of the cards are likely to refer less to ideas than to questions, or to actions that should appear on someone's "to do" list, but that will still leave a huge number of cards identifying at the very least the germ of a new idea.

What on earth do you do with all this stuff?

That's what wise evaluation is all about – how to select those ideas that the organization wishes to take through development and implementation.

EVALUATION IS A DECISION-MAKING PROCESS

Evaluation is about taking decisions – decisions as to which ideas to progress, which to shelve. And decisions are made by people – people who are subject to all the normal human pressures of politics, ambition, drive, fear, doubt. The objective of designing a process for wise evaluation is to ensure, as far as possible, that these natural human frailties do not get in the way.

When you decide to take an idea into development and implementation, you are doing two main things.

Firstly, you are committing resources – real resources that have costs, and that could be deployed elsewhere. A wise organization therefore wishes to be confident that committing those scarce resources to do "this" rather than "that" is commercially and organizationally the best choice. The ideal here is the "due diligence" test: imagine that in five years' time, some outside consultants do a study on your decision-making process – a situation that often arises in the public sector. If the consultants' report says "Given the information available at the time, the team took the best decision possible," then you have passed the due diligence test. For sure, as time evolves, new information comes to light, and new opportunities arise. But real business decisions have to be taken today, on the basis of today's information. So your aspiration should be to take the best possible decision in the light of the information available. That way, you and your colleagues can be confident that those resources are being committed wisely.

But however robust your decision making, you cannot foretell the future, and the idea might just not work out as you had hoped. For the second thing you are doing when you commit to development and implementation is to take a risk – things might just turn out differently. In taking your decision, you can't wish the risks away, or pretend they don't exist. What you can do, though, is to get as much insight as possible into the nature of those risks, and devise strategies to avoid them, or reduce their impact should they come to pass.

Wise evaluation is therefore all about providing a framework to help you and your organization make the best possible decision, so you can allocate scarce resources to best effect, in the light of as full an understanding of the risks as possible.

EVALUATION AS A BUSINESS PROCESS

The heart of wise evaluation is to select the "good" ideas from the "less good" ones in a timely and cost-effective manner, without creating a situation in which the originators of ideas – especially of those not selected – get demotivated, and say, "There's no point in suggesting ideas in this place – no one ever listens." Idea evaluation is in fact a business process, and can be designed and managed as such, as suggested in the next box.

THE SIX PRINCIPLES OF WISE EVALUATION

Transparency

The manner in which evaluation takes place should be open, accessible, fair, and intelligible. This avoids charges of nepotism or favoritism.

Completeness

The information used to support the evaluation decision must be robust, thorough, and complete, so that nothing of relevance can be inadvertently - or deliberately - overlooked.

Balance

No idea is perfect; no idea is all bad. Wise evaluation ensures that ideas are assessed in a balanced way, in the light of their benefits, their resource requirements, and their risks, in a spirit of constructive enquiry as opposed to adversarial hostility. This, together with completeness, ensures full professionalism.

Speed

Set performance measures as to the maximum amount of time that an idea, once formulated, can be "pending evaluation." What about one week for ideas that can be evaluated locally (within the department), one month for ideas that cross significant boundaries, and a maximum of three months for ideas that require much consultation?

Feedback

Don't keep the originators of ideas in purgatory. Make sure that the results of all evaluation decisions are fed back quickly to the originators, with explanations.

Pragmatism

Ideas are of all shapes, sizes, and qualities, so don't impose a single monolithic process, applied in the same way to all ideas.

THE EVALUATION SIEVE AND THE EVALUATION GRID

Some people envisage the evaluation process as a funnel (see, for example, page 102 of *The Age of Innovation* by Felix Janszen), but to me, this metaphor conjures up images of squeezing together, as things put in the "wide" end of the funnel get forced together before extrusion through the "narrow" end. Personally, I don't see the evaluation process quite like this: the metaphor I prefer is that of a series of sieves, with different mesh sizes.

EVALUATION AS A SIEVE

Imagine you have a pile of gravel, and your task is to separate out the different grades of stone sizes. One way of doing this is to use a series of sieves of progressively finer mesh sizes. The first sieve has a very coarse mesh, and when you put a shovelful of gravel on the sieve, and then shake it, all but the very biggest stones go through. The stones left in the sieve are the biggest, and they can be put in a neat pile. If the material that went through the first sieve is then shoveled into a second sieve, of a slightly less coarse mesh size, then the stuff staying in this second sieve is "size 2." This process can continue through as many sieves as you like, and the gravel gets separated by size.

Idea evaluation can be thought of similarly, with two main "sieves," which differ not in physical mesh size, but as regards the questions asked:

» **Sieve 1–"If this idea is implemented in full, what business benefit does it bring?"**
» **Sieve 2–"What resources are required to deliver this benefit?"**

There is also a third, subsidiary, sieve:

» **Sieve 3–"How radical is this idea?"**

The action of the first sieve is to separate ideas according to the likely benefit. I'm a great believer in simplicity, so initially I use just three categories – "high," "low," and "don't know." The second sieve separates according to the likely level of cost, and, once again, the three categories I've just mentioned are a pragmatic start. The third sieve separates ideas according to the likely degree of risk, in that a radical idea is probably more risky than an incremental idea.

INCREMENTAL IDEAS, RADICAL IDEAS, AND BLOCKBUSTERS

"We only want blockbuster ideas – ideas that are really radical!"

You've probably heard that – I certainly have, especially when a client is briefing me on what they want from an idea generation workshop. And when I hear it, I know I have a problem on my hands – or rather two problems, one of understanding, the other of expectations.

Let me deal firstly with the question of understanding – or, more accurately, misunderstanding. To me, the concepts of "blockbuster" and "radical" are very different. Yet they are often confused, and co-mingled. To me a "blockbuster" is an idea that meets with exceptional commercial or business success. Blockbusters can therefore be identified only after they have been implemented – we all hope for blockbusters in advance, but we can never actually know we have one until there is real, tangible experience of customer take-up (for a new product), or internal success (for a new process).

This is very different from the concept of "radical." To me, whether or not an idea is radical is a question of the features of the idea itself, and the degree to which these features are similar to, or different from, its antecedents and predecessors. If the new idea differs in only a few respects from its antecedents, then it is incremental; if in many, then it becomes increasingly radical. Whether or not an idea is radical is therefore a property of the idea itself, and the degree of "radicalness" can be assessed by comparing its features with those of the status quo as soon as the idea is well formulated, long before the idea comes to fruition. This comparison of features is, of course, facilitated by the *InnovAction!* process, especially if the process was used to identify the features of the status quo in the first place (see Chapter 6 of *Innovation Express*).

There is no law that I know of which states "all blockbusters are radical," nor one the other way round: "all radical ideas are blockbusters." Many blockbusters are, in fact, much more incremental than radical – sometimes ideas can be too radical in that the simultaneous change of a large number of features might be too much for the market to accept. "Radical" is a property of the idea; "blockbuster" is a term that can be applied only after the event, to describe how successful the idea is in practice. The two concepts are different, and should not be confused.

And since many incremental ideas can be enormously successful, I always try to set the expectation that success for an *InnovAction!* workshop is ideas of all sorts, the incremental being just as potentially valuable as the radical.

In principle, three sieves, each with three separation categories, give 27 possible combinations; in practice, not all of these require attention, for the purpose of the sieving process is to guide us as to where we should devote scarce resources of attention, analysis, and ultimately investment.

A very pragmatic, and relatively quick, process is therefore to take a batch of ideas, and apply the first two sieves, assessing each idea as regards benefits (high, low, don't know) and resources (high, low, don't know). Then, separate out those ideas with a don't know, and plot those remaining on a simple two-by-two "Evaluation Grid" (Fig. 3.1).

Ideas offering high benefit for low resources are archetypal "quick wins" – especially if they are incremental rather than radical – and should be authorized for implementation at once. Likewise, ideas offering low benefit for high resources should be shelved. But they shouldn't be lost, for circumstances might change – new technologies might become available which might radically reduce the resource requirement, or perhaps market conditions might change improving the benefit. At least once a year, and maybe twice, you should look through the list of shelved ideas to see if any should be reassessed – a

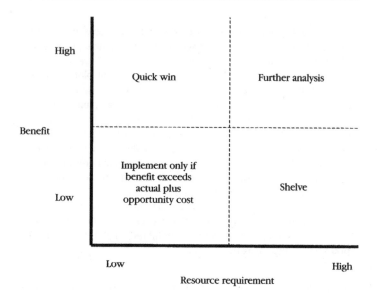

Fig. 3.1

formal process for doing this will be discussed in Chapter 7 on page 94.

Ideas offering low benefit for low resources might be worthwhile if the total net benefit package is sufficiently positive, if the risk profile is safe, and when the effort of introducing the idea does not distract people from more valuable tasks. Many ideas in this quadrant, however, will be shelved.

That leaves the most interesting quadrant – high benefit and high resource. These ideas are demanding, requiring high resources, but the effort of making these ideas happen might be a very good investment, for the benefits might be even higher. At present, we don't have enough information to take a decision, so these ideas warrant a more detailed analysis.

But what about the ideas that were associated with a "don't know" for either benefits or resource requirements, and so don't appear on the grid? This is a question of being pragmatic about how much effort is likely to be required to find out sufficient information to enable them to be plotted. There are no hard-and-fast rules here: if you consider that the effort is worth it, do it, and then plot the ideas on the grid accordingly; but if you have a good number of ideas in the "quick win" and "further analysis" quadrants, you may feel that you have enough to do to progress these. Once again, don't lose any ideas, but keep them for further review in due course.

The Evaluation Grid therefore acts as a robust and rapid way of categorizing ideas. Those that are quick wins can be actioned immediately; those that are shelved can be ignored, at least for the time being.

But what about those in the top right-hand quadrant? Those that need further analysis? That's what Chapter 6 is all about, but just before we get there, we need to look briefly at two other topics – the e-dimension and the global dimension.

The E-Dimension

This chapter makes the point that organizational culture is influenced by technology, but largely independent of it.

This is a very short chapter, for, to my mind, the influence of the e-world on organizational culture in general, and the cultural requirements for stimulating innovation in particular, are marginal. Organizational cultures existed long before the e-world came into being, and will survive long after the current e-craze is seen historically as just another step along the path of our increasingly sophisticated use of technology; likewise, humans have been innovative and creative ever since our species first evolved, and – I trust – will continue to be so for ever after! The key issues relating to creating an innovative culture therefore transcend "e."

Yes, as I describe in Chapter 4 of the companion title *Innovation Express*, the wiring of the world is having an enormous impact on the structures of industries and on the relationships between customers and suppliers, and so is acting as a tremendous spur to innovation in many ways. These changes will certainly influence organizational cultures, and organizational cultures themselves will determine how any single organization reacts to the e-stimulus, but to me the direct impact of the e-world on culture lies mainly in the domain of interpersonal communication.

The good news is that individuals in an organization have the potential opportunity to become much more connected, and this – as I describe in detail in Chapter 5 of *Innovation Express* and in summary on page 31 of the next chapter – is a major potential contributor to a very important ingredient in organizational creativity and innovation, an ingredient I call the *Brain Bank Connectivity (BBC)*. This is all about the creative power of connected brains, and captures the idea that two people working together can potentially be much more creative than the same two individuals working separately.

But you will have noticed my repeated use of the word "potential." Just because two people can send and receive e-mails far more quickly and easily than they used to be able to correspond by letter, fax, or even the telephone does not necessarily imply they are truly *connected*. The degree of interpersonal connectedness required to stimulate creativity is much more sophisticated than the ability to fire off a quick e-mail, or even to see the jerky movements of someone on a video conference.

As we all know from our personal experience, this degree of connectedness relies on interpersonal engagement, the mutual capturing and giving of true attention, and – most importantly – listening. These are very hard to achieve on the web.

So, to me, the e-world is largely peripheral to what I believe to be the essence of corporate culture – the interpersonal, the immediate, and the local.

The Global Dimension

This chapter argues that organizational cultures are local, not global, even in global organizations.

CULTURES ARE LOCAL, NOT GLOBAL

To me, cultures are local, not global.

Why do I say this? Because to me, culture is all about behavior, and behavior takes place when individuals are in contact with one another, immediately and locally.

That is not to deny long-distance, global influences – when I worked in Goldman Sachs, for example, as archetypal an American culture as you could imagine, I soon learned that there were all sorts of behaviors that Goldman regarded as culturally unacceptable, but were quite alright in my previous firm, Coopers & Lybrand, also an organization with a strong American influence, but a counterbalancing British one too.

The origin of the differences between the accepted – and indeed unaccepted – behaviors in the London offices of Coopers & Lybrand and Goldman Sachs is easy to explain. You can walk between these offices in a matter of minutes, but the two worlds are very different. Plumtree Court, the London office of Coopers & Lybrand at which I was based, was staffed almost exclusively by British people; all the senior management were British (some of them very "blue chip" indeed); and the office traced its roots back to the nineteenth-century British accounting firm, Cooper Brothers. Contact with our colleagues in the United States was sporadic and courteous.

A few hundred yards away from Plumtree Court lies Peterborough Court, the London location of Goldman Sachs. This office was set up by expatriate Americans when the firm wanted a presence in London. Most of the workforce is British, but when I was there, the great majority of the senior management was American, and contact with New York was very frequent indeed, partly driven by the needs of the business, but also driven by the direct managerial influence of the Goldman Sachs head office. To all intents and purposes, Peterborough Court in London's Fleet Street could have been in New York.

The American culture of Goldman Sachs in London was directly attributable to the presence of so many Americans in London and the more-than-daily contact with New York. And this was no accident – whenever Goldman Sachs open a new office (as they were doing systematically across Europe when I worked there in the early 1990s), a key decision was the choice of the founding team. These were always Americans, and they were known as "culture carriers."

Goldman Sachs knew that if they wanted to build a global culture, they had to do it locally by moving key people around.

Goldman Sachs also spend a huge sum of money on flying people all over the world, for they believe that the best way to build teams, to share knowledge, to build a cohesive international culture, is to get people together, in the same place at the same time. So the global culture becomes local.

FLOCKING AND THE *BBC*

Goldman Sachs's emphasis on gathering people together is in fact an example of "flocking" – a concept I discussed in Chapter 5 of *Innovation Express*. Flocking is a metaphor from the behavior of flocks of birds, which somehow seem to behave with a special coherence and cohesiveness as the flock soars, and changes direction, in the sky. In organizational terms, flocking – a term coined by Arie de Geus in his vivid book *The Living Company* – is the act of bringing people together, and he argues that this is the most powerful way of stimulating organizational learning.

Bringing people together, so forming direct connections between individuals, is of key importance in building a culture of innovation. By bringing people together, an organization can help build the organization's *BBC* – its *Brain Bank Connectivity*. I mentioned this concept briefly in Chapter 4 and I discuss it in detail in Chapter 5 of *Innovation Express*: its essence is based on the experience that most of us have had that the creative power of two people working together is usually larger than that of the same two people working individually. I'm sure you know what I mean – it's that magic moment when, during a conversation, the person you are talking to says something that gives you an idea. You describe it; the other person adds to it; and as a result the idea changes. After a brief dialog, a new, powerful idea emerges that neither of you would have had by yourselves.

That's the *BBC* in action. Because your brain was connected to another person's, you and that person together were able to generate a new idea that neither of you would have had individually. And so the creative power of yourself plus the other, connected, person is greater than the sum of the creative powers of yourself and the other person as individuals.

This additional creative power is a result of the *direct connection* between the two individuals, and so the total creative power of a group is attributable not only to the individuals themselves, but also to the number of active connections linking the individuals together. As I show in Chapter 5 of *Innovation Express*, the maximum number of connections between a group of people is a much bigger number than the size of the group itself: a group of four people, for example, has 11 possible connections - six connections between pairs of people, four connections between sub-groups of three people, and one connection linking all four people. So, if we ascribe one "creativity unit" to each individual and also to each separate linkage, then a group of four people working by themselves has a total creative power of four "creativity units," but a group of four people working together effectively has the potential creative power of 15 "creativity units"-11 for the linkages plus 4 for the individuals.

Organizations - like Goldman Sachs - that can harness the power of the *BBC* reap the reward. And they achieve it by ensuring that people are genuinely connected: connected by meeting one another, by getting to know one another well, by working with one another. And they do that on a global scale. By making the global local.

That said, the other issues relating to an innovative culture - issues like the way in which people are rewarded for generating ideas, the "rules of the game" for the allocation of budgets, and - very importantly - the way in which people behave in meetings when the most junior person suggests a new idea - are all truly local, happening right here, right now. Yes, they may be influenced by a "bigger picture," but if your boss's only reply to your bright new idea is "Don't be so stupid! How on earth could that work!?!," you know all about it here and now.

So the rest of this book will concentrate very much on the things that happen locally, and we'll start with looking at the state of the art for the most local of all: how ideas get evaluated.

The State of the Art

This chapter presents an approach to make the process of idea evaluation balanced and wise.

BALANCED EVALUATION

In Chapter 3, I introduced the Evaluation Grid, which acts as a pragmatic way of sorting ideas according to their likely benefits and resource requirements. As we saw, any idea in the top right-hand quadrant of the grid – one that requires high resources, but potentially delivers high benefit – is very likely to require further analysis before a decision can be taken to run with it, or shelve it. The purpose of this chapter is therefore to describe a powerful method for carrying out this analysis, a method based on some ideas originally proposed by Edward de Bono in his books *Six Thinking Hats* and *Six Action Shoes*.

Our objective is to design an evaluation process which meets the criteria shown in the box below by being robust, open, complete, fair, and, most importantly, balanced. De Bono suggested that these ideals can be achieved by examining an idea from a number of different perspectives, as represented by the wearing of six differently colored hats. I think it's useful to add a seventh (the purple one), too, and I summarize the roles of each hat, as I now use them, in the next box. Those familiar with de Bono's work will notice that my usage of the black and green hats is a little different from the usages originally proposed by de Bono: de Bono also tends to position his method as one of idea generation, whereas my method is firmly one of evaluation. Also, as you will see, the questions I associate with each hat are a natural extension of the three "sieve" questions, and so my form of the hats process builds on the work you will already have done in compiling the Evaluation Grid.

BALANCED EVALUATION

To evaluate an idea in a complete, fair, and balanced way, we need to examine the idea from a number of perspectives:

Benefits – Yellow hat
  What benefits will arise as a result of successfully implementing the idea? Who are the beneficiaries? What is the likely quantum of benefit? How long will it take for the benefits to come to fruition?

Issues to be managed – Black hat
What issues need to be managed to bring the idea to success? Which issues are potentially "showstoppers," and how can these be circumvented? What are the risks? And how can these risks be identified and managed?

Constituencies and feelings – Red hat
What constituencies (groups of people and individuals) will be affected by the idea, both when it is implemented, and also during implementation? What is their likely reaction to the idea? What can be done to manage these feelings to best effect?

Data – White hat
What data do we need to take an informed decision? What are the sources of the data, and how reliable are they? How do we handle uncertainty in the data?

Solutions – Green hat
What solutions can we identify to the problems identified by the black, red, and white hats? How can these problems be overcome?

Actions – Purple hat
What actions should we take in the light of our analysis so far? Do we have enough information to take a decision? Or is it appropriate to continue this analysis further?

Process – Blue hat
How do we orchestrate this process itself?

At first sight, the questions associated with the hats might appear clumsy and unnecessary – surely it's obvious when an idea is good or bad. Furthermore, the metaphor of the colored hats might be perceived as overly theatrical and trivial. Before you rush to judgment, pause for a while and try it.

As we saw in Chapter 2, many organizations do not formally evaluate ideas until a business case is tabled. But long before resources are committed to creating a business case for any particular idea, all sorts of informal evaluative processes have been invoked to eliminate the ideas that never come close to being the subject of business cases. How does this take place? In many organizations, it is either a question of power (only the boss's ideas get any daylight), or a modern-day equivalent of the medieval process of trial by ordeal – by definition, any idea (other than one of mine) is wrong, and the burden of proof is on the originator of the idea to prove it is "right," against all opposition. Those who believe in the tough, macho, survival-of-the-fittest school of management will consider this the best way to operate; my view is that it is wasteful, and decidedly unwise. So often, the macho school encourages shooting from the hip and jerking from the knee. The wise school, in contrast, encourages thinking from the head – and the head is the place where you put your hat.

The essence of the hats process is balance – rather than saying "you must prove your idea against all opposition," and so setting up an adversarial conflict, the hats process says "let's collectively examine the idea as richly as possible before we take an important decision." The process is therefore one of examination, exploration, and enquiry, and the standpoint is one of determining how to make the idea a success, rather than proving it will be a failure.

The metaphor of the hats is a mechanism to reinforce the nature of the process, and to help keep participants well focused. While we are wearing the yellow hat, we must focus on the benefits of the idea, and so must not drift off down other avenues; while we are wearing the red hat, we are exploring people's feelings. Yes, you can be theatrical, and wear colored hats, or sit in colored chairs, to emphasize the roles, but you don't have to: part of the role of the individual wearing the blue hat – the chairperson – is to remind people of the roles and to keep the discussion on track.

THE BENEFITS – YELLOW HAT

The yellow hat is all about benefits – what is good about the idea – and you should wear the yellow hat first. In many organizations, this is startling, for the most natural start to most discussions about ideas is to discover as many reasons as possible why they won't work. So to wear the yellow hat first introduces a spirit of optimism right at the start. In fact, you will already have been wearing the yellow hat when you asked the first "sieve" question, so you will already have some good information – the purpose of asking this question again is to take matters to a much more substantial depth.

WHO BENEFITS?

Wearing the yellow hat can often be good fun – most people get a buzz from thinking about benefits. When I am running groups wearing the yellow hat, I watch the bullet points appear on the flip chart, and after a page or two have been compiled, I ask them to note, by each benefit, who it is that is the beneficiary. As they go down the list, "us," "the company," "we do" begins to appear item by item.

"That's great," I say. "This idea clearly offers lots of benefits to you. But is there anyone else out there who might benefit too?"

"What do you mean?"

"Nothing much . . . I was just wondering if there are any people, other than yourselves and your company, who might benefit, that's all."

"Who do you mean?"

My preference at that stage is to shrug my shoulders and lift my eyebrows, hoping that someone in the group will get the point. So I pause, and – inwardly – pray.

"Maybe he's talking about people like our customers," says someone else, to my intense relief.

"And maybe our suppliers too ... and perhaps people in the local community..."

"What good suggestions," I chip in. "Why don't you spend a few moments thinking about people like customers, suppliers, the community, and maybe other constituencies too. Does your idea have any benefits to them too?"

And a few more pages of flip-chart are filled with benefits to others, benefits that they hadn't thought of, or noticed, until I prompted the thought. We all tend to be very self-centered, and inevitably we identify the benefits to "us."

It happens like that every time. But if you're alert to this, it won't happen to you. And, as a result, you'll identify a much richer package of benefits.

ISSUES TO BE MANAGED – BLACK HAT

The stance taken by the black hat is expressed by the question "What issues need to be managed to bring the idea to success?" These words are carefully chosen, for the starting point is the assumption that the idea can indeed be brought to success. In making this happen, however, a number of issues have to be managed along the way, and the purpose of the question is to identify what all those issues – and problems – are. Logically, of course, this enquiry is very similar to that initiated by "Let's have a really good time and find as many reasons as possible why Andrew's idea won't work," "This idea is stupid because . . ." and "Why haven't you thought of . . .?" – these too identify any number of problems and road blocks.

There are, however, two major differences. The first refers to completeness. The question "What issues need to be managed to bring this idea to success?" is seeking to identify all the problems likely to be encountered, so as to provide as comprehensive a picture as possible of what needs to be done, what resources need to be deployed, and what risks need to be managed. The more adversarial questions do not have completeness as an objective: rather, they are seeking to strike a killer blow – as soon as I can deliver a knockout punch, the fight is over. Such an adversarial frame of mind never examines all the likely problems, for the goal is that single devastating blow. If in fact the idea survives this assault, and a decision is made to go ahead, what usually happens is that all sorts of "unexpected" problems arise subsequently. Were they "unexpected?" Or was the original analysis weak?

The second difference between the two approaches is that of the viewpoint. The adversarial viewpoint takes the stance that the idea is bound to be a failure – all we need to do is to prove it to be so. This is very different from the stance of the question "What issues need to be managed to bring the idea to success?" Here we are imagining that the idea can work successfully, and that the task on hand is to be mature and insightful in identifying in advance all the things that might go wrong. By doing this, we can anticipate, and hence solve, the problems and manage the risks. This viewpoint is constructive and positive, rather than destructive and adversarial, and the difference between these stances is both profound and important.

As with the yellow hat, you won't be starting this process cold: much good information will be available from the work you did in answering the second and third "sieve" questions.

IT'S ALL ABOUT LANGUAGE

Those of us who enjoy a spirit of advocacy just love the game in which, if I can prove you wrong then this proves me right. Logically, of course, this is flawed, for the demonstration that one point of view is "wrong" is not evidence that any other point of view is necessarily "right" – both could be equally "wrong" or inappropriate. But we have all seen examples of this game being played throughout our organizational lives.

An important aspect of this game is our choice of language – we choose our words carefully, so as to maximize our chances of winning. I am a great believer that you can learn much about an organization's culture just by listening carefully to the words used in meetings and conversations.

Language is especially important as regards the use of the black hat. The role, as we now know, is to identify, comprehensively, all the issues that need to managed to bring the idea to success. Accordingly, the emotional standpoint of the black hatter is positive rather than negative, constructive rather than destructive. The black hatter is also politically neutral: neither an advocate nor an opponent; neither in cahoots with the idea's author, nor a hired assassin. When wearing the black hat, you should therefore try to avoid emotionally and politically charged language such as "the problem with this idea is that . . .," "this idea won't work because . . .," as well as the familiar put-downs "we tried that before and it didn't work . . .," "that may be OK for the competition, but we do things differently . . ." and the rest.

Far better to use phrases like "To make this idea work, we're going to have to ...," and "The learning we had from our most recent experience with something like this was ..." Questions such as "How can we avoid/solve/address [whatever]?", "What did we/others learn last time we did this?", "What other risks will we have to manage?" are good too.

FEELINGS AND EMOTIONS – RED HAT

The red hat is also seeking out problems, but from a rather different angle – the very personal angle of individuals and constituencies. The implementation of any new idea will inevitably affect people, and, at the end of the day, the success of the implementation is totally dependent on how people react to the idea and feel about the idea. This, of course, is particularly true of ideas associated with changes in processes, organization, and relationships. How many times have you heard "That idea didn't really work" or "That new process wasn't as big a success as we had hoped" or whatever? What, fundamentally, is the basis of these statements? Sometimes, the problem is technical – the technical aspects of the idea just didn't work. But in my experience, this is rare: far more likely, people – either as individuals or as groups – didn't end up behaving as the advocates of the idea wanted them to. Why not? Because, for whatever reason, they didn't want to, maybe because they didn't like the idea, or as a result of how the implementation of the idea was managed. We all know how to play organizational terrorist when we want to, and some of us are very good at it.

There is of course no law saying that everyone must like every new idea, and buy into it. Some ideas will inevitably cause some individuals or groups to be upset, perhaps because the change itself is perceived as an unnecessary upheaval, perhaps because as a result of the idea they are genuinely disadvantaged.

The purpose of the red hat is to identify, as comprehensively as possible, what these reactions might be like. In some ways, this overlaps with the black hat view, for these all represent issues to be managed. In many organizations, however, it is rare to consider people's feelings explicitly – in many macho cultures, it is taboo to think about feelings and emotions, for only wimps have feelings in the first place, and there are no wimps around here, are there? Well, I've been in some pretty macho cultures, and my observation is that the feelings *are* there – they are just not shown. The fact that the feelings exist still implies that people will respond in a variety of ways when their feelings are stimulated by the emotions that every human being experiences – fear, anxiety, approval, excitement, enthusiasm, whatever. It may be counter-cultural to let feelings be seen explicitly, but the resulting behaviors – blocking, defensiveness, evasion, political maneuvering, support, endorsement, alliances, deals, and all the rest – are usually evident in abundance.

The wise manager recognizes this, and knows the importance of managing all these issues. The benefit of the red hat is therefore making it explicit that, yes, people do have feelings, even if they don't show them overtly, and that it is wise to anticipate those feelings, and so devise strategies to overcome any resulting problems. The wise manager fully appreciates that a thorough red hat analysis can be instrumental in managing change effectively, and in making change stick.

FEELINGS MATTER

Partners in professional firms often have a high degree of independence and freedom, and this was particularly true when I was a partner in "old" Deloitte – that is, before its merger in 1990 with Coopers & Lybrand.

One aspect of this was the conduct of meetings. If the matter being discussed did not take my fancy, I could detach myself from the conversation – I would think about other things, doodle, look out of the window, make sure I avoided eye contact with others. I was not in any sense actively destructive, but I certainly was not on board. When the meeting was over, I could leave the table and did not feel bound by any agreements reached – I could go away and do my own thing. Sometimes, my detachment was driven by "intellectual" dissatisfaction, in which I could marshal cogent arguments as to why I was not in agreement, but more often, it was driven by emotion – I simply did not like the idea, felt threatened by it, or whatever. My actions would be driven more by emotion than by reason.

An aware meeting chairperson, of course, did not let that happen. She would notice my distraction, and deliberately involve me in the conversation – "Dennis, what do you think about that idea?" or even "Dennis, how do you feel about that idea?" would shake me out of my personal reverie, and oblige me to respond. I would not lie, and would articulate my dissatisfaction, causing me to reflect in my own mind as to the true nature of the discomfort. And usually, matters got resolved sensibly.

I don't feel any particular guilt in documenting this type of behavior – I suspect we have all had similar experiences. Feelings matter. And it is foolish to pretend they don't.

DATA – WHITE HAT

Most business decisions are better informed by reference to the appropriate data, and the role of the white hat is to identify what data is relevant. The data is usually required to quantify issues determined by the other hats, for example:

» As regards benefits:
  » How much revenue will be generated by the new product? What will the volumes be? What are the costs? And the margins?
  » How much money will be saved by introducing the new process?
» As regards issues to be managed:
  » How much will the change program cost?
  » What are the legal and regulatory issues?
  » What do we know about competitor activity in this area?
» As regards feelings and emotions:
  » How might we design a staff survey to find out their opinions?
  » How can we learn more about what our customers might think about this?

Questions of this type all have quantifiable or factual answers. Some will be established facts (such as those relating to legislation); some will draw on historic data (existing costs, for example); some will require forecasts (future revenue streams); some will relate to surveys (especially as regards feelings). All, however, are manageable, and all will contribute to the wisdom of the final decision.

In a more general sense, two white hat questions relevant to a new product are:

» How will it be used?
» What does it look like?

These questions can be answered in terms of a written description, and maybe a drawing or two. Far, far better, however, is a model, a prototype, something real. The closer an idea can come to reality, the easier it is to appreciate it, and to become enthusiastic about it. Making an idea real, in whatever ways are possible, is therefore an important contribution to the evaluation decision.

BLACK DISGUISED AS WHITE

The white hat seeks data, but the head wearing the white hat might have black thoughts in mind. It all depends on language, on tone of voice, and on body language.

I once worked with someone who smiled with his teeth, not his eyes. This confused me for a while, but not for long. Whenever, with a "smile," he asked, "How much is that likely to cost?" he was not making a factual enquiry, seeking to understand some data, he was making a highly emotionally charged statement. The emphasis on "that," the raised eyebrows, the knowing looks around the room to his political colleagues – all these signaled his disgust with the idea, and his contempt of the idea's originator.

On paper, though, the words constitute a legitimate white hat question; in actual use, the question is not a white hat question at all. Nor is the intended meaning a legitimate black hat question, for the black hat stance is one of assuming the idea can be made a success, and then discovering what we need to manage to make it so. The emotional stance for the black hat is positive and constructive, as well as realistic and feet-on-the-ground too; it isn't negative, miserable, destructive.

Wise managers are alert to malicious black masquerading as white, and never stoop to using this naïve ploy themselves.

SOLUTIONS – GREEN HAT

Many of the issues identified by the black and red hats will be problems, of greater or lesser significance. Often, these problems can be perceived as overwhelming, and so the role of the green hat is to allow some time and space for identifying solutions.

The key question asked by the green hat is therefore "How can this problem be overcome?" and the emotional stance is that this is in principle possible. Usually, the process invoked to answer this question is one of idea generation, and you can very successfully use *InnovAction!* (see Chapter 6 of *Innovation Express*) to identify and challenge all the assumptions in the normal way. The point to note here is that *InnovAction!* is not being used to generate new ideas in general, but rather to identify new ideas very much focused on solving a specific problem, which itself has been identified in the context of exploring a "bigger" idea.

As an example, suppose the idea being analyzed using the "hats" process is to develop a new product, and that the black hat has identified that an issue to be managed is the need to go to full 24-hour, three-shift working. It is also likely that the red hat analysis will have identified that "our staff won't like the disruption of three-shift working." This could be seen as an overwhelming problem, a true blocker. But the job of the green hat is to tease out solutions to the problem, such as a new incentive package, revised agreements with unions, recruiting from different sources (such as students), or sharing staff with neighboring businesses – even competitors. There is no law saying that any of these potential solutions will work, or will be cost-effective, but their exploration keeps the matter open, and – you never know – you might come up with a very good solution.

ACTIONS – PURPLE HAT

The role of the purple hat is to ask "What next?" The overall purpose of evaluation, remember, is to lead to a decision as to whether or not an idea is to be taken into development and implementation, and the role of the hats process is to structure the gathering of supporting evidence so that this decision can be taken wisely. One of the benefits of using the hats is that the process can be as modest or as extensive as is appropriate – it is quite possible to carry out a hats analysis in an hour or so; you can also use the hats framework as the basis for a fully documented business case or feasibility study, which might take months. To devote months of effort, however, costs money, and so the role of the purple hat throughout the process is to ask, from time to time, "What do we do next? Do we have sufficient information to take a decision, or is it worth continuing this analysis to a deeper level?"

MAKING DECISIONS

As I have stressed many times throughout my discussion of evaluation, the ultimate objective of evaluation is to take a decision – do we proceed with this idea or not? Decisions are taken by people exercising judgment, not by systems following algorithms. The whole purpose of the hats process for balanced evaluation is to provide the decision-making body – an individual, or a small group – with appropriate, balanced, comprehensive information on which that judgment can be based. But at the end of the day, the decision is taken by people, and the decision is based on human judgment.

ORCHESTRATION – BLUE HAT

The final hat is the blue one – as worn by the person chairing or orchestrating the process. The role here is quite straightforward: to determine how the process overall will be used, and to keep it on track. In my experience, this is usually very easy to do. The process itself is simple, and it is extremely rare for anyone to object to either its underlying motive – balance and wisdom – or its method – to examine an idea from a multiplicity of angles. What I find amazing is the willingness with which people "play the game" – even the most died-in-the-wool black-hatters, who have never been heard to say a good word about anything for the last umpteen years (I'm sure you've met him!), will amaze both themselves and everyone else that, when they are asked to put on a yellow hat ("just for once"), they do so, and at last say something positive. It works. It really does.

EVALUATION IN PRACTICE

BUSINESS CASES

Take a look at your business's guidelines for producing business cases and feasibility studies – perhaps you can find a recent example of the finished article, or maybe you have access to some guidelines. Compare the structure of your document to a structure derived from the key questions of the "hats" process:

» What are the benefits?
» What are the issues to manage?
» How will people feel?
» What data do we need to take a balanced judgment?
» What solutions are there to the problems identified?
» What do we do next?

If you do this, you will probably find that there is a lot on the benefits – business cases are always written by advocates, and advocates always stress the benefits. You will also find stacks of data, from market projections to detailed analyses of costs, from NPVs to IRRs. In good business cases, you will also find at least some analysis of risk. But – in my experience – the risk analysis is often relatively shallow, and there is rarely an explicit analysis of feelings and emotions.

One of the strengths of the hats framework is that it can be beneficially used at all stages in the evaluation process from the initial idea, right through to the full business case – the difference lies in the depth of the analysis, not the breadth.

A GOOD IDEA THAT BACKFIRED

Many businesses actively seek to encourage everyone throughout the organization to have ideas, and to put them forward safely. This benevolent thought often translates into a suggestion scheme, whereby individuals are invited to submit suggestions, either by putting a slip of paper in the box in the staff canteen, or, these days, by e-mailing the Innovation Center.

What might happen next?

Well, people are motivated and excited (good), and feel empowered (even better), and put lots and lots of ideas into the scheme (which was the scheme's objective, so this is great). This flood of input comes to the central team of two people, who have been asked to look through the ideas, and select the "good" ones. The two people in question also have a day-job to do, and so take some time to look through the suggestions, which continue to come in daily. This processing delay means it takes some time before any decisions can be taken, and before there is any feedback to the originators. Before too long, there is a rumor on the shop floor, "Don't bother suggesting anything – nothing ever happens, and no one ever tells us what's going on!" and the scheme is discredited from below.

But worse happens from above. When the team of two look through the suggestions to produce the short list to refer to senior management, senior management take the view that short-listed items are "trivial," "impractical," and "not appropriate at this time," thereby confirming their view that only they can have any good ideas.

And so the well-intentioned suggestion scheme slowly slides into oblivion, and the cynics congratulate themselves that, once again, they were right.

This anecdote is real, and many organizations have started off with the best of intentions, only to be disappointed. With, admittedly, some degree of hindsight, let's do a quick hats analysis of this particular way of encouraging people to suggest new ideas. So, the proposition we are evaluating is:

"We intend to introduce a suggestion scheme in which individuals are encouraged to put forward new ideas. Individuals will write their ideas on a form, and submit them either on paper or by e-mail to the Innovation Center. The ideas will be sorted, feedback will be given, and the best ideas will be taken to a committee of senior managers for approval. We will also reward the best ideas."

EVALUATION IN PRACTICE

Think about this proposition for a few moments, and do a quick yellow, black, red, and white hat analysis. Then choose two or three of the most difficult-looking problems, and put on the green hat for a few moments to see if you can come up with some solutions.

Here is my list of benefits:

» The scheme will result in more new ideas than we had otherwise.
» Some of these ideas might have significant business impact.
» The scheme will encourage people throughout the organization.
» The scheme sends all the right messages about the importance of innovation in our business, and how everyone can contribute.
» People throughout the business will feel pleased with a more positive climate.
» Those who get rewards will feel good.

And here are some issues to be managed:

» How can we design a process so that ideas are handled quickly, both in terms of selection and evaluation, and also in providing feedback?
» How can we ensure that the feedback is constructive, and that those whose ideas are rejected don't get discouraged themselves, and don't discourage others?
» How will we manage a situation in which, after an initial splurge of suggestions, things might just dry up?
» How will the Innovation Center judge which ideas are "good"?
» Will that judgment align with that of the senior management panel?

» What if the senior people don't like the ideas selected by the Innovation Center?
» How will we judge who gets a reward?
» What form will the reward take?

These are some red hat issues:

» The workforce might feel:
  » good because of the encouragement;
  » good because they can suggest ideas in a much more direct way then hitherto;
  » discouraged if they get slow feedback;
  » let down and misled if they get no feedback;
  » disappointed if one of their own ideas is rejected;
  » elated if one of their own ideas wins an award;
  » jealous if one of someone else's ideas does . . .
  » . . . and maybe suspicious and critical of the criteria by which awards are determined;
  » under threat if they believe that the number and perceived quality of the ideas they personally suggest are being used in some way as a measure of their personal performance
  » . . . and maybe confused if they feel they haven't been trained in how to generate ideas.
» The staff at the Innovation Centre might feel:
  » good because this raises the profile of innovation in general, and their role in particular;
  » stressed if they are inundated with a large number of ideas quickly;
  » disappointed if the flow of ideas is modest;
  » under threat if their performance is measured by the number of ideas . . .
  » . . . and angry if their performance is measured by the perceived quality of the ideas, which, by definition, are not theirs, but other people's;
  » good if the senior management panel endorses the ideas they put forward . . .
  » . . . but under threat if they don't;
  » unfairly treated if the workforce blame them for anything they don't like.

» And the senior managers might feel:
>   » skeptical, especially if "we've tried that before"...
>   » ... alternatively, excited by the prospect of empowering everyone to come up with new ideas;
>   » very pleased if at least some of the ideas they are given to review are perceived as "good"...
>   » ... alternatively, frustrated or angry if they believe that the ideas they are given to review are "trivial," and that all the time and money devoted to the scheme has been wasted.

The white hat might identify the need:

» to assess the volume of ideas likely to be generated, and how this might evolve over time;
» to determine the criteria for judging, at the Innovation Center, what constitutes a "good" idea, and agreeing those criteria with the senior managers;
» to determine the criteria for judging which ideas are to win an award, and how that judgment may be seen to be taken fairly.

This analysis took about 20 minutes to think through and note down, and, even for such a simple-looking idea, it does identify quite a few points that aren't so simple. Central to the whole concept is the question of what constitutes a "good" idea – what might appear to be a good idea to the idea's originator might be judged trivial by a panel of senior managers. If this happens just occasionally, then there is unlikely to be a problem; on the other hand, if this happens to most of the suggestions, then the whole concept very quickly becomes discredited.

Time for the green hat. What ideas can we generate to address the problem of inadvertently stimulating a whole host of "trivial" ideas? One way of doing this is to use the *InnovAction!* process on the core of the idea itself, two particular features of which are:

» the proposal focuses on the suggestion of ideas;
» the proposal encourages individuals to suggest ideas.

How might these be different?

Well . . . suppose the proposal were to encourage not the suggestion of a "raw" idea, but the suggestion of an idea which has been through at least an initial evaluation process. So, instead of just suggesting an idea by itself, the material that is put forward is accompanied by an initial hats analysis. That way, the originator is obliged to think beyond the raw idea, and consider the benefits, the issues, the feelings, the data. The originator can then take a much more balanced view, and submit only those ideas that have been taken at least one step beyond the initial suggestion.

This richer concept can be taken further by considering how "the proposal encourages individuals to suggest ideas" might be different. Suppose the concept was one in which teams, rather than individuals, were encouraged to come up with ideas. How might this work?

Well, suppose that an individual has a bright idea. Rather than putting that idea straight into the suggestion box, the idea originator is encouraged to convene a small group of, say, three or four people they feel comfortable with. The role of this small group is to carry out an initial hats analysis, on the basis of which they take a collective decision whether or not they feel the idea is strong enough to put forward to the more formal process. If they collectively decide it isn't, the matter is dropped there; if they decide it is, they fill out a brief set of forms, one describing the idea as a whole, and then one page each for benefits, issues, feelings, data, any other related ideas, and recommended actions. This pack is then submitted to the Innovation Center (or wherever), and it is this pack that is reviewed.

What are the benefits of this, enriched, process relative to its predecessor?

Several. Idea generation continues to be encouraged, but a much more rigorous process is encouraged at source. This will result in fewer ideas being passed through (so reducing the workload at the Innovation Center), but those ideas that are passed through are likely to be of much better quality, since they will have had some initial analysis. This initial analysis is carried out locally, in safety. Because this first level of evaluation is being carried out by the originator, and some people the originator trusts, if in fact the local team decide not to progress the idea, the originator is much less likely to feel aggrieved or damaged. The process has been conducted "in private" rather than "in public," so there should be much less of a concern that the originator is being "judged"; furthermore, the process is being carried out quickly and locally, not slowly and remotely. And most importantly, because the originator is sharing the initial idea with other people, it is most likely that the idea itself will become enriched as a result of the contributions of others.

There are, however, two important issues to be managed to make this work. The first is that people need to be trained in both idea generation and idea evaluation, so they can generate new ideas, and apply the hats process, with confidence. Secondly, people must be allowed the time to convene the local groups to carry out the evaluation, and this time must be allowed for in budgets, in work practices, and in performance measures.

How much training is required? How much will this cost? And how can we estimate the time to be allowed for the local groups? This is all good white hat stuff, and needs to be assessed. And, not forgetting the red hat, the most likely reaction of local management is to resent the time being taken, possibly at short notice, to convene the local evaluation groups. This then leads to the green hat idea that maybe this can be incorporated into normal working practices, so it is not seen to be something special. Many organizations – especially in manufacturing – already have mechanisms such as quality circles or continuous improvement teams, so why not dovetail this process alongside these very similar initiatives?

WHAT ACTION WOULD YOU TAKE?

You have now read about two alternative ways of introducing a staff suggestion scheme: one in which individuals are encouraged to put ideas straight into the suggestion box; the other in which individuals are encouraged to discuss their ideas with a local team, then do an initial hats analysis, and only when the local team are confident do they submit the idea into the formal process.

Which of these two would you choose to adopt? Or, if neither, how would you design one?

This invites you to wear the purple hat, and take action. Which did you choose? Why? As you will have noticed, the text of the last few pages has been an iterative hats-style exploration on the basic idea of a suggestion scheme. What started as a bright idea ("let's have a suggestion scheme") was constructively examined using the hats, and enriched to encourage local teams rather than individuals, and to have as its output not just a "raw" idea, but an idea that has been subject to some initial, rigorous analysis. So, if you feel that this process added value to your own thinking, why not use it for real?

Innovative Cultures in Practice

This chapter answers the question "What distinguishes an innovative organization from an uninnovative one?", and describes the two "big things" that need to be in place for your organizational culture to be innovative, the "five important motivators" to encourage your staff to be innovative, and the "five fundamental organizational enablers" that help make it all happen.

CULTURE IS ALL ABOUT PRACTICE

Cultures don't exist in theory – they exist only in practice. So this chapter deals with the heart of the subject, and – unsurprisingly – there is quite a lot to say! This chapter is therefore rather longer than the others, and is structured in three main parts:

1 an examination of the key features that distinguish between an innovative organization and an uninnovative one;
2 a discussion of the five important motivators that act as incentives for individuals to display their creative and innovative talents to the full:
   » the role of senior management
   » performance measures
   » reward and recognition
   » training
   » embedding innovation into the day-job;
3 a description of **five fundamental organization enablers** that equip the organization as a whole to make innovation happen:
   » the physical environment
   » budgets
   » project funding
   » managing projects
   » managing the pipeline of ideas.

WHAT DISTINGUISHES AN INNOVATIVE ORGANIZATION FROM AN UNINNOVATIVE ONE?

Our starting point is a question: what is it – precisely – that distinguishes an innovative organization from an uninnovative one? This is exactly the question asked by James Christiansen, who spent three years researching this issue, publishing his findings in two highly informative books, *Competitive Innovation Management* and *Building the Innovative Organization*, from which I learned a great deal.

It would make life easy if the difference between innovative and uninnovative organizations could be boiled down to one or two key factors along the lines "Innovative organizations do X and Y, and uninnovative organizations don't. So, if you want to become an innovative organization, all you have to do is fix X and Y, and everything will be fine." Unfortunately - and as I'm sure you expect - life is more complex than that: the difference between the two types of organization isn't attributable to just a few characteristics, rather:

HOW TO MAKE INNOVATION HAPPEN

To make innovation happen, you need two big things, and lots of little things.

Let's take a look at just what is involved.

WHAT ARE THE "TWO BIG THINGS"?

If you want to make innovation happen in your organization, the two big things you need are:

» firstly, the will to do it;
» secondly, some financial "headroom."

The will to do it is, in a word, all about leadership. To make innovation happen within your organization, some things will have to change: maybe it's the reward system, perhaps it's the way budgets are allocated; maybe the criteria for promotion, perhaps the overall attitude to risk. Whatever it is that needs to be changed, introducing the change, pushing it through - and making it stick - all demand every ounce of all the familiar characteristics of leadership: being able to paint and articulate a compelling vision of how much better the future will be by having moved from "here" to "there;" building the right political consensus; keeping things going when they get tough. This is all hard work, and we all have a day-job to do. So don't embark on this course of action if you don't have the will to see it through. Far better not to start, than to start and fail.

The second "big thing" I call financial "headroom." An absolute certainty about making innovation happen within an organization is that it is going to cost money and demand people's time. At the very least, money will be needed to finance activities such as training, feasibility studies, and idea development, and time needs to be spent on idea generation, evaluation, development, and implementation. Much of this time and money will have no immediately "provable" return, for, as we have seen at length, the early stages of innovation are exploratory, while the later stages of development and implementation are always subject to the risk that, at the end of the day, the new idea will not prove to be as powerful as we had all hoped.

All this money and time has to come from somewhere. And that "somewhere" is of course the same pot that is funding the advertising budget, the new head office building, the e-business project, and the replacement of the factory machinery. And that pot might be very small, especially if the business is in trouble. One of the unfortunate truths in business life is that some organizations wake up to the fact that innovation is critical to business success far too late, asking the question "How can we become more innovative?" just at the time when they can't afford to do anything about it.

HOW MUCH SHOULD YOU SPEND ON INNOVATION?

I am often asked "How much should our innovation budget be?" My initial answer is usually along the lines "If you sincerely believe, as I do, that innovation is the ultimate competitive advantage, then you should budget as much as you can afford, and put in place a number of processes to ensure that the money and time are spent wisely."

In practice, there are two ways of establishing what the budget might be, bottom-up and top-down. The bottom-up approach is to identify all the activities – training, travel, meetings, feasibility studies, market trials, prototyping, whatever – that are likely to consume time and money, estimate the quantum for each of them, and add all the numbers up. The alternative is to work top-down, and ask the question "How much can we afford to spend?" This is in essence a question of looking at the overall budget, and asking the directors to come to consensus about how much of that can be spent on an activity which is unlikely to give a return in the current year, and, at worst, might give no directly traceable return at all. This highly polarized approach certainly tests the will to do it! But, if the will is there, this can result in the agreement of a figure, which can then be used to allocate against various individual activities.

In my experience, organizations that are in the earlier stages of becoming innovative benefit more from the top-down approach: it is quicker, more pragmatic, and achieves the objective of ensuring that at least some funds – however big or small – are earmarked for innovation. As the organization gains more experience, and people begin to see that there is a return on the expenditure – as manifest by an improved flow of ideas and their corresponding visible results – then innovation becomes progressively more well established as "the way we do things around here," and so becomes embedded in the normal budgeting process.

Ideally, of course, the will to do it, and the budgetary approval, come from the very top, for it is at the very top that power converges to a single person or a small group. If he, she, or they collectively have the will, they too have the power to allocate funds and to make it happen. In practice, however, the will and the funds do not have to come from the very top – a lot can be done from a local top, such as at business unit or even departmental level. It is of course harder to do things locally, for "to get away with it" you need at best the protection of your immediate boss, or at worst an agreement of benign non-interference – if your boss actively intervenes to stop it happening, then it won't.

So, let's assume that these "big things" are in place . . .

WHAT ABOUT THE "LOTS OF LITTLE THINGS?"

These refer to a host of policies and procedures, all of which will be familiar to any organization: policies and procedures relating to ten broad themes falling into two main categories – **motivators**, which actively motivate and encourage people to be innovative themselves, and to encourage innovation in others, and **enablers**, which create the conditions that enable innovation to happen:

1 Motivators
   » The role of senior management
   » Performance measures
   » Reward and recognition
   » Training
   » Embedding innovation into the day-job.
2 Enablers
   » The physical environment
   » Budgets
   » Project funding
   » Managing projects
   » Managing the pipeline of ideas.

In an innovative organization, all the detail underlying these main themes has been deliberately designed to encourage, support, and reward innovation, so that all aspects of the business are consistent and pointing in the same direction. In an uninnovative organization, it is rare that the detail has been designed deliberately to prevent innovation, for few people are sufficiently malicious and powerful to achieve that. Much more common is a situation in which various aspects of the detail are inconsistent and pointing in different directions – not because a malevolent force designed them like that, but rather because different policies evolved at different times. Well-intentioned efforts to become more innovative therefore become frustrated because the myriad of detailed policies are inconsistent.

An example. Suppose you have a great idea about how your business unit might collaborate with another in the group to develop a new product. You go to the boss of your business unit, and you are puzzled that he is lukewarm. Is he deliberately trying to kill innovation? Perhaps he is. But suppose that his performance measures reward him for his business unit's profits, and that his bonus depends primarily on this – a totally normal situation in most businesses. Your proposal might be a jolly good idea, but since it crosses business unit boundaries, the benefit of the idea does not accrue to your (and your boss's) business unit exclusively. And if your boss has the choice between backing your project, and another, which in a wider sense might be less exciting, but which delivers benefits to your business unit exclusively, which would you expect the boss to choose? Your boss is behaving totally rationally by supporting the other project and rejecting yours. The issue is not that your boss is deliberately trying to kill your idea – rather, there is a (probably inadvertent) conflict between the performance measures applied to your boss, and the fact that your idea happens to cross organizational boundaries.

A moment's thought, of course, will show that it is most unlikely that this organization will ever discover anything useful about how different business units might collaborate, for it is in no one's interests to do this. In a general sense, this might be considered a "bad thing" – although many would argue that this is neither a good thing nor a bad thing, it's just the way things are when you give managers clearly defined local objectives.

But things don't have to be that way – they can be designed differently. In relation to this example, suppose you can approach the Group directly for the funding of your idea – and approach them in a way that does not look like you are going behind your boss's back. Group, in fact, might have money available specifically for funding projects which cross organizational boundaries, for they realize that such projects will not get funding within their local business units. This gives the best of both worlds – local business unit bosses can maximize the profits of their units as well as supporting innovation locally, while Group provides funds for cross-business unit innovation.

This solution, of course, won't just happen by itself: it has to be thought of, and implemented – an example of both process and organizational innovation: process innovation in creating the mechanism whereby Group can allocate funds, and organizational innovation in making it safe for people working in any business unit to have direct access to Group. It is simply a question of making different aspects of business policies and procedures mutually consistent and supportive of innovation.

Nor is this solution "rocket science": it is a very straightforward approach. But that doesn't stop it being powerful, for there are many businesses today that suffer from the problem of being unable to sponsor cross-business innovation.

How to build an "unlearning organization"

The next two main sections will therefore look at some of the detail underpinning the 10 themes mentioned on page 56, dealing firstly with the motivators and then the enablers. Since "unlearning" is the central feature of idea generation (see page 4, and also Chapter 6 of *Innovation Express*), I call an organization that has all of this right an "unlearning organization."

So as to set your expectations correctly, what follows is not, by any means, rocket science – rather, it is all "common sense." Also, the distinction between "motivators" and "enablers" is not rigid, and, as you will see, there are many ways in which the two interact.

So, let's see how to build an unlearning organization. . .

MOTIVATORS

The five themes

This section will explore the five cultural themes classified on page 56 as "motivators":

» the role of senior management;
» performance measures;
» reward and recognition;
» training;
» embedding innovation into the day-job.

The role of senior management

Senior management have an enormously important role in determining whether or not an organization is truly innovative – largely because they have the power to make things happen, or to block things they don't like. In many organizations, managers are promoted on their ability to get things done, and to deliver successful results on time, within budget. Typically, these are the skills associated with the outer implementation zone, rather than the innermost zone of idea generation. Senior people who are strongly task-oriented and results-driven can often be intolerant of the more open-ended, exploratory, and ambiguous style associated with that magic question "How might this be different?" (see *Innovation Express*, Chapter 6). This does not necessarily mean that innovation is stifled: most senior managers are intelligent, and can understand its intellectual framework. They may not like it personally, but they are usually wise enough to "let it be" for others.

But even if the top guys and gals do understand it, their role is not simply one of allowing idea generation to happen by looking the other way - there are many other areas in which senior managers have an influence.

Take promotion, for example. Senior managers will often sit on assessment centers or selection panels, and they will groom their successors. The criteria for promotion may or may not be published, but the results certainly are: whenever an individual is promoted, their unpromoted former peers, and hoping-to-be-promoted subordinates, will spend hours working out just what it is that Lucy has that caused her to get promoted. Senior managers have promotion in their gift, and the criteria used in practice are highly visible. Is the key to promotion success in the day-job, delivering a steady operating result, and beating the budget by just enough to be seen as a good manager, but without being given a hugely stretched target in the next year? Or is it to be seen to have taken a "risk" by working on an innovative project, outside the day-job's normal line structure? Senior managers who say the right words about the importance of innovation, but who are seen to groom and promote those who play safe, are creating around themselves an environment in which two important levers - what senior management says and what senior management does - are pointing in different directions, with the inevitable result that people will take their cue from the actions, not the words, and play safe. Innovation surely won't flourish here.

Similarly, senior managers have a strong influence on budgets and the allocation of funds. If it's a struggle to get the budgets for training, or for bringing people together for idea generation workshops, then once again innovation will wither. That's not to imply that innovation requires profligacy and a general lack of financial control. On the contrary, financial control is a "best practice" discipline for innovative organizations too. The issue is the allocation of funds in the first place, and their protection thereafter - activities associated with innovation do require money, and that money should be made available without the necessity of wringing blood out of stones.

That leads to yet another role of senior management in innovation - protection. Innovation, as we have seen on many occasions now, is a fragile flower, and one of the most beneficial acts of senior

managers is to protect innovative activities – especially idea generation – until they have borne fruit; they should not press for evaluation
too soon, and they should protect the idea from being evaluated by
others prematurely; they should also ensure that the time meant to
be spent on innovation is actually spent – for example, by creating a
context in which middle managers fully understand the importance of
idea generation sessions, and do not stop their staff attending because
of some panic with the day-job. These are all everyday signals that
innovation is important, and, as usual, the opposite behaviors – such as
condoning absence at training courses, or allowing people to be pulled
off innovation projects at short notice – send very strong signals about
what is, and what is not, really important.

Senior managers also play a vital role in resolving cross-boundary
conflicts, such as those associated with creating inter-disciplinary teams,
or providing access to information. The most exciting innovations are
often at or over boundaries (see, for example, Chapter 5 of my book
Unlock Your Mind), and senior managers have it in their power to
make that happen, or to block it.

And finally in this section, there is the role of senior managers in
mentoring, and story-telling. Who are the heroes in your organization?
And what is the nature of their heroism, the basis of their esteem?
Senior managers, by virtue of the stories they tell, the role models
they advocate, the praise they bestow, send any number of signals
about what the organization really values. If innovation is part of
the story, this becomes very visible, and everyone seeks to emulate
those behaviors. But if it isn't – despite the mission statement and the
corporate advertisements – they won't.

So, the role of senior managers is pervasive and subtle. If they
are sincere advocates of innovation, and active participants in the
process, great. But if they aren't, merely sitting back and letting it
be isn't quite enough: they must ensure that they don't – probably
inadvertently – send out all the wrong signals in lots of other ways.

PERFORMANCE MEASURES

All managers know that even if it has been budgeted for, it doesn't
necessarily happen – that's what monitoring and control are all about.
And the heart of monitoring and control are the systems of performance

measures, and the (hopefully corresponding) systems of reward and remuneration. I'll talk about reward structures in the next section: let me deal with performance measures here.

To me, performance measures are the fundamental drivers of behavior: if I have a choice between two actions, I will take that action which is most likely to contribute beneficially to my performance measures. So, if a key performance measure is this period's profit, I will avoid taking actions which might jeopardize that objective, even if the action I fail to take might have improved next period's (or, more likely, some more future period's) profit. Or if a more subtle performance measure is the extent to which I can keep my immediate line boss happy, I will seek to do that, and decline activities such as working on a "special project" for someone else.

This is of course all familiar stuff, and alert managers know all the rules of this particular game. But when an organization is seeking to become more innovative, this will not happen in practice until some practical and realistic performance measures are in place, and layering in yet another set of objectives and measures makes life even more complicated.

These complications arise in three ways: time, method, and consistency.

The issue of time is simple: innovation is not a quick-fix, and the benefits of becoming more innovative evolve relatively slowly. Any organization seeking to become more innovative will therefore incur the costs and the pain long before they see benefits, and this cuts across all the everyday, period-by-period measures. Introducing performance measures that encourage and nurture innovation inevitably gives rise to conflict with those designed to encourage short-term performance, and squaring this particular circle requires thought, consultation, and leadership.

The issue of method is less simple, and relates to what, precisely, you want to encourage, and therefore measure. The endgame, obviously, is business success, and this comes from the implementation of good ideas. This leads to the identification of output measures such as revenue attributable to new products, cost savings attributable to new processes, or whatever – measures that focus on the end result of the active and successful management of the whole Innovation Target.

But, as we all know, it takes time for this to happen, and so there is another set of performance measures which apply to the management of the Innovation Target itself – measures such as the number of new ideas generated; the number of ideas submitted for evaluation; the speed of the evaluation process itself; the number of ideas accepted; the number of ideas in development; and so on.

And in advance of the measures of the process are a series of input measures such as the amount of time spent on idea generation, the number of people trained and skilled in creativity and innovation, and the amount of time spent on evaluation.

And in addition to all of these, there are any number of behavioral characteristics that an innovative organization might wish to encourage – such as sharing knowledge, participating in teams, coaching innovation in others, being willing to accept the ideas of others – some of which can be measured relatively easily, others less so.

So many things we could measure – it's all overwhelming.

The immediate tendency, particularly of task-oriented folk, is to focus on output measures such as the profit attributable to new products. This is indeed a valid measure, but my experience is that this works well only in relatively sophisticated environments, which are culturally very attuned to innovation, and already have a well-stocked pipeline of ideas – the archetypal example is 3M who, as described in Ernest Gundling's recent book *The 3M Way to Innovation*, have a performance measure that 30% of the sales revenue in any one year is attributable to products that were not in the catalog four years before.

For organizations that do not yet have that degree of maturity with respect to innovation, my suggestion is that you introduce an increasingly rich portfolio of measures steadily over time, starting with input measures (most importantly, number of people trained in creativity and innovation, and the amount of time devoted to idea generation and evaluation), then moving on through the process measures (monitoring the flow through the idea pipeline), and only then introduce output measures. By adopting a staged approach, you reduce complexity, you minimize the burden of new systems, and you are most likely to stimulate the activities and behaviors you really wish to encourage.

The issue of consistency is more complex still – this being a question of how the objective of encouraging innovation can have an effect on performance measures throughout the organization. Suppose, for example, that you wish to stimulate innovation, perhaps as a pilot project, within a particular business unit – say, in a particular territory. You do all the right things, getting the business unit's leadership on side, agreeing the budgets, training the people, and encouraging idea generation. Suppose further that the boss of that business unit wants to back a particular idea, and seeks funds and approval from his own boss, who perhaps is managerially responsible for three territories.

But let's further suppose that the performance measures of the "big" boss have remained unchanged. What might happen? In a word, conflict – perhaps inadvertent, but conflict nonetheless. When the business unit boss seeks approval for something risky, which delivers benefits across organizational boundaries, but not for some years yet, as we have already seen, the "big" boss might take the view that this particular project does not meet his own objectives, and so turns it down.

This is just one example of the more general issue that the performance measures in one part of the business might not be fully aligned with those in another part of the business. As businesses grow and change, this can happen very easily, by accident. But one of the "little things" that an innovative organization gets right is to ensure that performance measures across the entire organization are mutually consistent.

REWARD AND RECOGNITION

The subject of performance measures leads naturally to that of reward and recognition: if we wish to encourage innovation, then surely those who contribute to it should be rewarded accordingly. Yes, they should, but – as often happens in this complex area – there is quite a lot to think about, the top six topics being:

» Should there be a special reward for innovation ("Innovator of the Year"), or should the reward be incorporated into the remuneration package?
» Who gets rewarded – individuals, or teams, or both?

» What form does the reward take?
» Who judges?
» According to what criteria?
» And what about sanctions and failure?

Special rewards

The first topic – special awards or rewards as part of the normal remuneration package – is a false dilemma: it is not a question of either/or but of both ... and. Special awards are, by definition, public, and can become part of the folklore of the business, for the recipients of the award become heroes. This fits in with some organizational cultures, but not all, and the key issue to bear in mind is visible fairness – the recipients of such awards are necessarily relatively few, and all must be seen by their peers as deserving of such an award. Rewards as part of the remuneration package are public in that the existence of the reward as part of a bonus package will be well known, but – in most organizations – the amount awarded to any one individual will be private, and ought to be consistent with actual performance in the context of the agreed performance measures. There is also no exclusivity here: literally everyone in the organization can receive an element of bonus, if they deserve it, and if the profits are there to be shared around.

Individual or team?

Innovation, at any of the four stages of idea generation, evaluation, development, and implementation, let alone as regards the whole sequence, is almost never a solitary activity, and so to identify a lone individual as the recipient of a special award inevitably will disadvantage some people who will have contributed. The issue here is to strike a balance between, on the one hand, being seen to encourage innovation, and also to offer a reward to a deserving individual, and on the other, being seen to be fair. My experience is that public awards to individuals should be modest in value, but high on prestige (more value can always be assigned to the annual bonus), so as to avoid unhelpful jealousies and accusations of unfairness; public awards to small teams are in my view better, but even with a team award, there will always be someone on the outside. Most importantly, you must avoid the situation in which only the "boss" is eligible for the reward: bosses do not always deserve the credit for what was done by their teams.

What form of reward is best?

The form of any recognition for innovation also merits attention, for money, shares in the spin-off company created as a result of commercializing the idea, promotion, or benefits-in-kind (the all-expenses-paid two weeks in the Caribbean) have value to some, but not to all. Some people value time more than money, or a degree of independence, or the opportunity for some form of sabbatical break, perhaps for education, perhaps to spend time in another organization, perhaps to play golf. Christiansen, in *Competitive Innovation Management* (pages 158-9), starkly contrasts 3M, which allows individuals to spend up to 15% of their working time on projects of their own choosing, to "Northern Pharmaceuticals" (a pseudonym), whose employees "are expressly forbidden to work on their own projects, their time being 100% allocated to corporate projects." Which organization is the more innovative? You guessed. 3M.

Who judges?

Special, public awards need to be seen to be fair, so the judgments need to be made by, ideally, a panel of trusted people; rewards as part of the remuneration package are subject to the same rules as other elements of an annual bonus – usually, this is determined by the line boss, ideally after consultation with those in a position to give an informed view. This is where the performance measures come into the equation – I too have played the game "I did this, this, and this in accordance with my performance measures, so my bonus should be x." If an individual feels there are any disconnects between what he or she believes was done, how it was measured, and how this mapped on to the bonus actually awarded, then my experience is that their behaviors are driven by what was actually received. So beware the situation in which staff are exhorted to be innovative, but those who judge fail to recognize it.

What are the criteria?

These issues discussed so far are complex enough, but the most vexed concern the criteria for any award, from the public prize to the personal bonus. Is it a question of ideas generated – in which case, what about ideas that turn out to be very half-baked indeed? Is it a question of ideas that achieve commercial success – in which case, how long to you have to wait until this is determined, and what are the criteria of success? And what about ideas that aren't about specific new products, or those that reduce the costs of processes, or ideas that don't influence either revenues or costs directly – ideas about relationships, organization, or strategy? And what about those people who haven't necessarily come up with ideas themselves, but who have created a context or an environment in which others have flourished? And what is the balance between rewarding outcomes and effort? Maybe it is appropriate to be seen to be rewarding well-intentioned endeavor, even if the outcome is as yet unknown, or even a "failure." This is deep water indeed, and I know of no magic, universal answers. But wise managers aren't daunted by these types of real-world issues: the important matter is to be well aware of the issues involved, to assess them in the context of your specific circumstances, and to be as wise as you can.

What about sanctions and failure?

Before leaving this section, let me dwell for a moment on two related topics – sanctions and failure. Sanctions are less talked about than rewards, but they too play a role in making explicit what types of behavior an organization wishes to encourage, and discourage. I'm not talking here of building a culture of fear, or of penalizing people by withholding pay or benefits, but of the way in which individuals are alerted to problem areas, and the importance of ensuring that bonuses are true recognitions of achievement, rather than automatic outcomes of having survived another year.

Failure, too, is another tricky subject, especially in the context of innovation. Innovation is inevitably risky, and to me that means that things can genuinely turn out differently from what we might have hoped. Is this "failure?" Perhaps; but perhaps not. To me, the key issue is the distinction between negligence and genuinely unforeseen circumstances. No one can foresee the future with certainty, and so, in deciding to proceed with a new product, for example, no one can guarantee that the product will be as unique as we had all hoped, and reach the sales targets to which we all aspire. But you can, and should, take into account all available data, and you can and should identify all possible risks, and devise strategies and tactics to mitigate them.

Not everything we try is going to be successful – innovation is all about risk. But if people associated with a project that did not work out as well as we had hoped – even though they did the best they could possibly do – are seen to suffer as a consequence (by being sidelined, being passed over for promotion, having their salary held or even cut, or being fired), then the signal this sends to everyone else in the organization is very powerful indeed. Don't take risks. Do the day-job. Keep your head down. So, the issue of rewards is not just about rewarding those who get it right – it's also about being wise to those who appear to be getting it "wrong" too.

TRAINING

Innovation and creativity are skills that can be learned, but since the conventional educational systems do not teach them, it is up to organizations to remedy this in their internal training activities. Innovation and creativity are therefore important components of a wise organization's training and development programs. Once innovation is well established as a natural part of the "way we do things around here," this program is likely to comprise a series of "master classes" to keep people refreshed, as well as some induction training for new joiners, but for organizations seeking to move from "here" to "there," there will be a backlog of skill enhancement that needs to be addressed by means of a special training initiative.

Who should be included in this program? And how might it take place?

My answer to the "who" question is "everybody" – everybody can contribute to innovation, and I see no reason why anyone, from the receptionist and the catering staff to the managing director and chairman, should be denied the opportunity. But I also recognize that different people have different levels of interest, so a series of different programs makes sense, with each module within the overall program specifically targeted at, and designed for, a particular community.

One community is that of the top management. I've already discussed the importance of their role in innovation, and they can only do that if they have the appropriate knowledge of what innovation is all about.

In my experience, it takes about three hours to brief senior managers to the required level of insight, and this ideally takes place in a half-day session, either convened specially for this purpose, or embedded within a broader event.

There are many ways of delivering an organization-wide training program, but one that you might like to think about is to identify three further communities beyond top management:

» **specialists** – those people likely to have a particular interest in creativity and innovation, and who will act as local champions;
» **facilitators** – those people who have not only a particular interest, but can also act as facilitators and trainers of local groups;
» **participants** – everybody else.

Specialists need to be fully confident in the tools and techniques of innovation, and require a training program of at least two days, so that they can deal with matters in the appropriate depth. As a result, they should be well equipped to lead, and contribute to, idea generation workshops, and the evaluation process.

Facilitators need this level of training, and even more so. Many aspects of innovation, especially idea generation, are best carried out in small groups, and these usually benefit from active facilitation. Those who play the role of facilitator need to have not only skills and confidence in facilitation in general, but also a deep knowledge of creativity and innovation. The facilitator training courses I run usually take about five days, which allows time for simulations, video training, and plenty of discussion on how best to conduct *InnovAction!* workshops (see Chapter 6 of *Innovation Express* for more on *InnovAction!*).

Those who are neither specialists nor facilitators are participants – encouraged to come up with ideas and to participate in idea generation and evaluation, but with no especial responsibilities. To play this role, people certainly need a modest level of training in the tools and techniques, so that they are equipped to participate, rather than to lead. In addition – and perhaps more importantly – people must be given a very clear and sincere message of encouragement, and assured that they are genuinely invited to participate in creativity and innovation. Part of this message is a clear explanation of how the innovation process works in your organization, so that people know what to do when they have an idea; how to suggest, be invited to, and participate in *InnovAction!* workshops; how the evaluation process works, and their potential role in it; and how participation in the innovation process is related to their appraisal and development, and to the remuneration and reward system.

This requires, of course, that all these organizational processes have been designed and implemented: this seems obvious, but it is not always the case – some organizations, with the aspiration of raising the levels of both skill and enthusiasm for creativity and innovation, launch significant training programs focusing on creativity tools and techniques, but without having first ensured consistency across the accompanying business processes. This training, of course, is fun and exciting, but it does not have the intended effect. If the organization has not built the processes for managing the pipeline, for wise and balanced evaluation, for funding and staffing projects, and for reward and remuneration, then what happens after people have been enthused? They start generating ideas, only to discover that there is no process for dealing with them; those ideas that do get evaluated may not be evaluated quickly and fairly; and people soon find that the systems for performance measures, reward, and remuneration remain unchanged, and make no recognition of the new emphasis on innovation. The result of all this is disillusionment and distrust as another management fad bites the dust. This is doubly bad news – the failure of the training initiative to deliver the required results is bad enough, but even worse is the deep discrediting of innovation as a fundamental organizational goal, so making it even harder to implement innovation the second time around.

So, be wise, and don't confuse energy with effectiveness. Resist the pressure to roll out an organization-wide training program until all the other aspects of the innovation process are fully in place.

EMBEDDING INNOVATION INTO THE DAY-JOB

The ultimate objective of creating a truly unlearning organization is to make creativity and innovation a natural feature of everyday existence, a totally normal aspect of "the way we do things around here." Innovation isn't something "special," something we go away to do at off-site meetings, or is the unique preserve of that department – where is it now? – oh yes, somewhere in marketing I think. Or did I hear that they closed it down last year? I'm not sure ...

Wise organizations and wise managers embed innovation in the day-job, and they incorporate the tools and techniques, and the process, in the things that happen every day. They rejoice in it, they give it visibility, they publicize it. Take a look at your organization's internal newspaper, and see how many articles there are celebrating the success of innovation. Not too many? And how often does your organization get calls from the press or Business Schools asking for case studies?

The easiest way of embedding innovation into the day-job is to start using the language of hats, at meetings and in conversation. "That's rather a black hat remark," "Let's all wear our yellow hats to think about the advantages of that suggestion," and "If I wear my red hat, I don't think I like that too much" are all perfectly natural statements, once the organization has sanctioned the use of the metaphor, and people have some insight as to what the color-coding means. The *InnovAction!* process too can be used whenever there is a problem to solve, no matter how humble. All that needs to happen is for people to recognize that compiling a detailed description of what happens now is a very powerful way of helping people to ask, and answer, that magic question "How might this be different?"

Every organization, for example, is involved in some way or other with IT in general, and system and process design in particular. Although process reengineering may be rather less fashionable now, the processes of redesigning old systems and designing new ones will continue into the indefinite future. Take a look at the work-plans your organization has used for some recent design projects, and ask these questions:

» What did we actually *do* with the maps we drew of the current process? Did we use them to ask, systematically, "How might this be different?" Why not?
» Have all our systems designers had formal training in innovation and creativity so that they can apply the tools and techniques with confidence on all our system and process design activities? Why not?

In my view, innovation and creativity should be an intrinsic part of the thinking of all IT professionals, and tools such as *InnovAction!* should be standard components of the IT function's methodology. Given the ever-increasing role of technology as a source of competitive advantage, and the dependence of the rest of the organization on the quality of the IT team, this might be your view too.

Another opportunity relates to quality, where concepts such as total quality management, continuous improvement, and lean manufacture, supported by processes such as quality circles, are well established in many organizations, especially in manufacturing. The essence of all these initiatives is to strive for better processes, and encouraging those intimately associated with the processes to discover these improvements for themselves. As described in the next box, *InnovAction!* is totally consistent with this approach, and can inject additional energy and enthusiasm into what by now might perhaps be a somewhat tired process.

INNOVACTION! AND QUALITY CIRCLES

Many manufacturing organizations have gained great benefit from the various quality initiatives that have been developed over the past 20 years or so. One of the most powerful is the "Quality Circle," in which small groups, usually of shop floor operatives, are encouraged to improve their own processes and methods by working collectively to solve local problems. There are any number of tools and techniques to support this, such as Ishikawa's fishbone diagram (to help break a more complex problem down into its constituents), and the "Five why's" (if you ask the question "why?" repeatedly – rather like a challenging television interviewer tackling a particularly evasive politician – you will probably discover the underlying truths, as well as the assumptions that you rarely challenge).

The *InnovAction!* process is totally consistent with these, since its starting point is a complete description of what happens now – a description which will be in harmony with, and probably more complete than, the descriptions elicited by fishbones (which tend to describe what's wrong, rather than what is) or the five why's (which tends to seek explanations rather than descriptions). Where *InnovAction!* adds new value is by encouraging the team to ask "How might this be different?" systematically for all the features – even those where there is no explicit problem to solve, but where a better way might be discovered.

Quality Circles have been used with success at shop-floor level in manufacturing industry, but it is very rare to find similar processes operating in other sectors, or in functions such as marketing or accounting, and even rarer at middle and senior management levels. Do these parts of the business have no opportunity for improving their efficiency and effectiveness? I wonder.

One activity, for example, that is very much within the domain of top management is strategic and business planning. There are many methods to support this fundamentally important process, and one of the most powerful of these – to my mind – is known as scenario planning. As I describe in the next section, the *InnovAction!* process can play a very natural role in this vital activity.

INNOVATION AND SCENARIO PLANNING

Strategy formulation is itself one of the domains in which innovation can be enormously valuable, and there are three different ways in which innovation might be relevant:

» as a *result* of strategy formulation, in the sense of defining a strategic vision, and the corresponding actions, which are innovative as compared to your actual and potential competitors;
» as a *goal* of the strategy, in the sense of making innovation, and the creation of a truly unlearning organization, a strategic objective;
» as applied to the *process* of strategy formulation itself, so that this is done in an innovative way.

There are many ways of formulating strategy, and the business bookshops have many shelves full of books which will give you advice on how to do it. The process I wish to discuss here is called scenario planning, a brief overview of which is given in the next box.

SCENARIO PLANNING

Scenario planning evolved during the 1960s as a result of the activities of Herman Kahn, at the American think-tank, the RAND Corporation; Peter Schwartz, at Stanford Research Institute, at that time a department of Stanford University in California; and Pierre Wack, at the industrial giant, Shell. All were grappling with the fundamental problem underpinning all planning: how can we best take decisions which are inevitably long lasting, when the future is in fact uncertain?

One approach is to attempt to remove the uncertainty by better prediction and forecasting: if only we can be "cleverer," then we can eliminate the uncertainty, and our decisions and plans will work. A second, diametrically opposed, approach is to assume that prediction is impossible, and that the best approach is to take short-term decisions, and to revisit them continually, adjusting them as circumstances change.

Scenario planning takes a middle course. It rejects the "we can predict" school as intellectually unsound, and the "we are powerless" view on the grounds that it can degenerate into the abdication of all managerial responsibility. The central tenet of scenario planning is that, although no one can predict the future with certainty, it is very possible to imagine a variety of possible futures which might come to pass. Each of these can be used to test various strategic policies and actions, and from this, the management team can agree upon which policies and actions they wish to take, but with a very profound insight into the corresponding risks and uncertainties.

Scenario planning itself has several associated methodologies (as described, for example in *Scenario Planning: Managing for the future* by Gill Ringland, and *Scenarios: The art of strategic conversation* by Kees van der Heijden); central to the one I use is a table, the structure of which is represented in Fig. 7.1.

The columns represent "worlds," with the first column being "today's world," and the remaining ones possible alternative "future

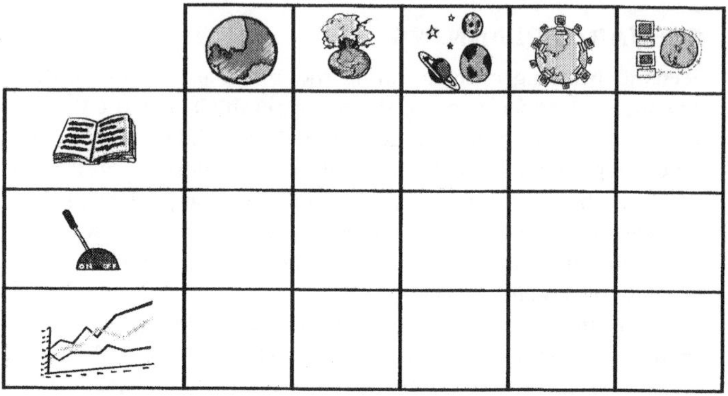

Fig. 7.1

worlds''; the three rows represent, respectively, "descriptions,"
"levers," and "outcomes."

Let me explain this by reference to the first column, "today's world."
In the "description" row, the top left cell represents a complete
description of the external context in which a business or organization
operates – a description encompassing the current commercial and
industrial structure, the nature of competition, the legislative and
regulatory framework, the technological environment, and so on.

The "levers" row contains information relating to the "levers" that
managers can pull, which reflect their decisions. These levers have two
attributes: "names" and "settings." For example, one lever might have
the name "staff establishment," and a setting of "3250," indicating
that, as at today, the organization employs 3250 people. This number is
a matter of managerial choice – depending on the strategy and policies
of the organization, there could be more or fewer people. Other levers
will represent, for example, products, services, channels to market,
pricing policy, and the like – collectively, the total set of levers reflects
all the various decisions that managers can take.

The "outcomes" row contains information relating to the outcomes
of the business, once again expressed in terms of "names" and
"settings": as an example, one outcome might have the name "total

sales revenue" and the setting "£5 billion." Other outcomes represent profit, market share, share price, credit rating, reputation, staff morale, and so on, so that the total set of outcomes reflects all the results of running the business.

Overall, when completed, the first column represents "today's world," showing a comprehensive description of what that world looks like, a list of the levers and their settings, and a list of the outcomes and their settings. This captures the essence of what is happening in the business today: in the existing world, by setting our levers at particular chosen positions, we achieve the resulting outcomes.

So much for "today's world" – what about the "future worlds?"

Let's assume for the moment that we have compiled descriptions of some possible, but very different, "future worlds," and that we have populated the entire top row of the table – how we can do this I shall describe shortly. The reason I skip over this for the moment is to demonstrate how this table, when completed, can help determine strategy.

Suppose for the moment that the levers stay at their current "today's world" settings in all the identified "future worlds." Having compiled a description of each world, you can ask the question "If my levers are at their given settings in a particular 'future world,' will the outcomes be favorable or unfavorable?" If you have a good insight as to what a particular "future world" might look like, as achieved by having compiled its description, this is in fact an easier process than it might seem: it can be done by group discussion, or by analysis, for example by using models. If the answer is "favorable," then fine. But if the answer is "unfavorable," then this prompts the question "What do the lever settings have to be to create a favorable outcome in a particular world?" This too can be assessed by discussion or by analysis, and results in a process in which the lever settings are "reverse engineered," perhaps by trial and error but more likely by applying careful thought, to give a favorable set of outcomes in the chosen "future world."

If this process is repeated for each "future world," the table can be completed: each column contains a description of each world, associated with the settings of the levers which the management team believe will give favorable outcomes. In general, the lever settings will be different in each "future world," and that's why formulating strategy is not easy – if it didn't matter what decisions you take (as manifest by the settings of the levers), then we'd all have a very easy job indeed.

How, then, do you determine the strategy? By discussing with your colleagues which lever settings you collectively believe in. And the completion of the scenario planning table makes this discussion very well informed: it acts as a "laboratory" against which you can test ideas, policies, potential actions. And as a result, you can agree which actions to take, for, at the end of the day, the strategy can only manifest itself as a series of actions in which you choose to move selected levers from "here" to "there" – there is nothing else that a manager can do.

CONNECTING LEVERS TO OUTCOMES

Levers represent management actions, for the *only* action a manager can take is to reset a lever from one position to another: you can hire more staff, you can retrain others, you can advertise more, you can open up new markets. These are all examples of resetting levers – the staff number lever, the skill lever, the advertising lever, the market lever.

Outcomes represent the results of these actions – the sales revenue outcome, the profit outcome, the share price outcome.

Unfortunately, there are no levers with outcome names such as "sales revenue," "profit," "share price," and the rest, for there are no actions managers can *directly* take to influence, for example, sales. The connections between the levers and the outcomes are indirect: you hope that by advertising more, market share will increase; you hope that having better-trained staff will increase customer satisfaction and hence sales. And to make matters even more complex, there are also all sorts of time lags between taking an action (in the current jargon, resetting a lever), and the hoped-for result (a beneficial outcome).

It is therefore a profound truth that *no lever is directly connected to any outcome*, and it is this absence of direct connections between the levers (what managers can actually do) and the outcomes (what managers want) that makes managing the challenge it indeed is. Yes, levers and outcomes are linked, but the linkages are indirect, complex, subtle, sometimes in mutual conflict, and often time-lagged. How, then, should all the levers be set to give optimal outcomes?

Good managers have an intuitive understanding of how the levers and outcomes are linked, both logically and over time. But even the best managers have learned that they can supplement their intuition with "systems thinking" - a powerful tool specifically designed to tame the complexity of understanding how the settings of all the levers determine the values of the various outcomes. Systems thinking is also the basis of "system dynamics modeling," a computer-based simulation modeling technique that can be used to explore how complex systems evolve over time.

Systems thinking and system dynamics modeling can play a very valuable role in scenario planning, for they can help specify how your levers are linked to your outcomes, under a variety of contexts, as defined by "today's world" and the various alternative "future worlds."

The process I have outlined does not require any prediction, for it does not require that the management team divine which one of the alternative "future worlds" will in fact come to pass. Nor is it a process in which managers place a bet, totally blind. Rather, it's a process in which the management team can thoughtfully and rigorously imagine what alternative "future worlds" might come to pass, and, as a result, determine policies and strategies in the full light of the inevitable uncertainty. And it does something else too - by creating a context in which managers can explore the future, by building what the scenario planners vividly call a "memory of the future," the management team is alerted to the way in which the future might evolve, so that as time actually evolves, you can be very alert to changes in the external context, you can spot the early signs of change long before your competitors, and you can react accordingly.

The heart of the process, clearly, is to imagine the "future worlds." How in practice is this done? Let me now answer this question, which I skipped over a few paragraphs ago. By using *InnovAction!* of course!

The first row in the scenario planning table represents a detailed description of "today's world," and the various alternative "future worlds" – descriptions of the context in which your business operates now or might operate in the future, expressed in terms of the commercial and industrial structure, the nature of competition, the legislative and regulatory framework, the technological environment, and so on. These descriptions can be formulated as a (very long!) series of bullet points, structured under various appropriate sub-headings.

The description of any "future world" must, of course, be different in some way from that of "today's world" – if it wasn't, the two worlds would be indistinguishable. And the easiest way of assembling sets of different descriptions is – you've got it – by asking "How might this be different?" of each of the bullet points in the description of "today's world." *InnovAction!* in action! That's why the first step in the process is to compile a good description of "today's world" – it's always best to start with what you know.

For sure, with a large number of bullet points in the description of "today's world," the process of asking "How might this be different?" can generate a huge number of alternatives. Also, during this process, it is very valuable to involve a broad range of people, including external technical experts, who can provide specialist knowledge as well as contributing to the collective imagination. Yes, after a short while it does get a mess, and, somewhat later, there are so many different possibilities on cards plastered all over the walls, it appears to be totally chaotic. But with reflection, the ideas cluster, and some self-consistent descriptions of possible "future worlds" emerge – the human brain is extremely good at organizing this sort of material.

InnovAction!, then, can lie at the heart of an innovative strategic planning process, and that's another way of helping embed creativity and innovation into the day-job – in this case, the day-job of the most senior managers.

EMBEDDING INNOVATION INTO THE DAY-JOB

Imagine going into an organization, and seeing on the walls of the marketing department, a factory, the IT department, or wherever, long lists of "features of the way we do things," these being bullet point descriptions of how we manufacture our products, deliver our service, do our pricing, negotiate with suppliers, treat our

staff, or whatever. And imagine further a banner right across these saying "How might we do this differently? Please discuss new ideas with your colleagues, and e-mail your 'hatted' ideas to. . ."
What stops this from being your organization?

Summary

Well, I've covered a lot of material in this section, but it's important stuff: I trust the mind map shown in Fig. 7.2 will help as a succinct summary of the main themes.

ENABLERS

The five enablers

This section examines the five enablers (see page 000):

» the physical environment
» budgets
» project funding
» managing projects
» managing the pipeline of ideas.

The physical environment

When you visit an innovative organization, you can immediately sense the energy, the drive, the buzz. Much of this comes from the people and the way they behave, but the physical environment is important too, and many organizations have gone to some trouble to create their environments to be as encouraging of innovation as possible.

No, it isn't a 1960s hippy paradise, with psychedelic patterns on the walls, bean-bags on the floor, and strange aromas in the air. All the innovative organizations I know are well disciplined, hard-working and commercially aware. But they pay attention to detail, and they take care. They appreciate the importance of natural light, and having the temperature well controlled. They provide their staff with appropriate, and up-to-date, technology. They know that people require privacy,

Fig. 7.2

and quiet – often solitary – spaces where they can work, and be able to concentrate without interruption. They know too that you need communal spaces where meetings and workshops can be held. And they also know that much innovation happens by chance interaction – two people happen to bump into one another accidentally, and have a conversation that, totally unexpectedly, results in a fantastic idea. So they don't leave such opportunities to chance – they deliberately design their environment to make such "accidental meetings" happen. How? Here are two ideas:

» Have a rule that bans internal telephone calls and – more importantly – internal e-mails within any single building. That way, you have to go to see the person you want to communicate with, and who knows who you will meet on the way.
» Do not position people who naturally work together next to one another. If you normally work with someone, you will seek them out. If you sit next to someone you don't normally work with, new networks will soon get built.

For sure, it's hard – and in practice unrealistic – to apply these rules absolutely rigorously, but that's not the point. The point is to design your environment to encourage people to interact with each other, and to maximize the likelihood of having different people meeting one another by chance.

One of the most important places where people meet is over a meal. So take a look at your staff restaurant or canteen and ask whether or not it is an environment that is conducive to people being innovative. In most houses, the kitchen is the hub: it's warm, the family can eat and drink there, it's the center of communication. Is your staff restaurant the hub of your organization? Why not?

BUDGETS

Innovation costs money, and this must be budgeted. Nothing is more frustrating than the statement "We can't take that initiative, we didn't budget for it." With innovation, of course, you can't predict – and therefore you can't budget for – specific, pre-identified, ideas. But you can predict, plan for, and allocate budgets to, specific activities: in general, an innovative organization will spend money on:

» training, including:
  » innovation in general, and idea generation and evaluation in particular;
  » other related topics such as systems thinking, project management, risk analysis, and risk management;

» how innovation works in your organization;
» communication, teamwork, and culture;
» communication:
    » within the organization, to share ideas;
    » externally, to gather information from the outside world;
» knowledge transfer:
    » to help the "brain bank connectivity" (see page 31);
» idea generation:
    » primarily an allowance for workshops;
» idea evaluation:
    » to allow for all stages of evaluation from local, team-based evaluation, through feasibility studies, to fully fledged business cases;
» development and implementation:
    » for projects which pass through the evaluation process;
» rewards:
    » for example, to reward new ideas;
» pipeline administration:
    » managing the pipeline of new ideas is possibly a new business process, and needs funds for creation, and then ongoing operation.

How much should be allocated to each? Clearly, there are no generic answers – it all depends on context. But what does not depend on context are the headings. So take a look through your budget, and see if sums of money, and time allowances, have been earmarked for each of these activities. Every manager knows that if it hasn't been budgeted for, it won't happen.

PROJECT FUNDING

This sounds simple: once you commit to innovation, you have to make funds available for projects, particularly feasibility studies and development projects. In practice, though, it can be clumsy, especially if an organization perpetuates its capital allocation procedures from its pre-innovation days.

Some thoughts to bear in mind, which correspond very closely to many of the themes explored in our discussion of evaluation, are:

» Not everything has to go to the Main Board for approval

Funding can be made available throughout the organization, at different levels, for appropriate amounts, for projects of differing scales and risk profiles.

» Make decisions quickly

Innovation does not ripen with age, so make funding decisions as quickly as possible once there is a robust enough proposal.

» Make decisions close to the idea's origin

This is desirable not only as regards speed, but also to avoid distortion of the message. If the funding source for an idea is a long way from its origin, the likelihood is that the approval process passes through many hands – and minds – on its journey from originator to funding authority. At each intermediate point, the idea can suffer from dilution, distortion, and a progressive loss of enthusiasm and passion.

» Don't forget to make provision for funding organizational "orphans"

These three points collectively suggest a funding framework whereby sums of money to support innovation can be made available throughout the organization – this makes the processes local (and regional), fast, and close to the points of origin. In all likelihood, this will reflect the organization structure. That's fine, and this devolved process should work well for those ideas which naturally fit within the objectives and performance measures of that structure. But some ideas won't naturally "fit" – they might relate to cross-organizational new products or processes, or ideas that are simply too big for any one organizational unit to handle. There is therefore a danger that these ideas become "orphans" – potentially good ideas, but ideas that don't readily have organizational champions in a devolved structure. As we have already discussed (see page 85), a wise organization anticipates this, and makes funds available specifically for such ideas: in addition to the funding process aligned to the formal organization structure, different levels of the organization (say, Divisional and Group) have pots of money available to be allocated to ideas which would otherwise risk being lost as orphans.

MANAGING PROJECTS

Here is a conversation you do not overhear in an innovative organization:

> "Did you hear about Pat?"
> "No. What happened?"
> "He's been assigned to a special project."
> "He's on his way out, then!"

Innovative organizations understand the importance of running both their line structure, and also a project structure, in parallel and in harmony. The line structure is there for continuity, and for delivering day-to-day operations; projects are there for special, one-off activities. Most innovation activities, before they become fully developed, fall into the project category, and for innovation to be successful, the organization must be able to create and manage project teams, lasting from a matter of just a few days, to many months or perhaps even a year or two.

The main difference between the line and a project concerns time: the line is in essence timeless, running in perpetuity, whereas projects have a finite time span, and have a definite start and end. This implies that, for a project to be successful, the project team must be convened, then managed, and ultimately disbanded. It is here, of course, that the main difficulties arise: the line and project teams both demand the very best resources, and if, as in almost every organization, "best" resources are in short supply, the demands of the line and the demands of projects are in direct conflict. The conflict can arise in many ways, for example:

» Departmental line managers can be reluctant to allow members of their team to be seconded to projects – why should a line boss release their best people?
» Individuals being asked to join project teams might be reluctant to do so, for all sorts of reasons – perhaps they feel that their lines of patronage for their next promotion will be broken; perhaps they fear that their line boss will feel they are being disloyal by their "resignation"; perhaps they are worried that their line job will no longer be available when the project is finished; perhaps they just don't want to take a risk in case the project is not seen to be a

gleaming success (and we all know what happened to the last guy who volunteered for a failed project, don't we?).

Under conditions like these, the departmental manager, and the person invited to join the project team, can cement an alliance whereby "I'm very sorry, but I just can't leave the line job." The result of all this is that the project gets staffed by rejects – all those people whose departmental managers are pleased to see the back of them – and the likelihood that the project will be a success is severely jeopardized. And if the project does indeed turn out to be a failure, those who managed to avoid having been associated with it congratulate themselves on their lucky escape, and vow never to work on a project in their careers. No wonder the organization can't innovate.

Staffing innovation projects with the best people is probably the single most powerful, yet most difficult, action to achieve, since it goes to the heart of the organization. What, then, do wise organizations do? Lots of things, things like . . .

- » ensuring that career progression is seen to include time in the line as well as time on innovation projects;
- » building career development programs which incorporate line time and project time – although you can't predict what the nature of an innovation project might be in three years' time, an innovative organization will have full confidence in saying that "in about three years' time, you should plan for about six months on an innovation project";
- » incorporating sensible succession planning so that there is never a problem whenever a particular person is seconded out of the line;
- » ensuring that the reward structure for project participants recognizes their contribution to innovation projects, and is not unfairly harsh as regards "failure";
- » ensuring that the reward structure for departmental managers recognizes their role in nurturing innovation and creativity in others, and in allowing their staff to move out of line roles;
- » ensuring that people are not "out of sight, out of mind" while on projects;
- » ensuring that, towards the end of a project, people are successfully reintegrated into the line.

As we have seen so often now, none of this is rocket science – it's all no more and no less than managerial common sense. But it all needs attention, and if an organization is not used to staffing projects, these topics all work consistently together to help make innovation happen.

What about the project itself? As Martin Barnes, an eminent project manager, once said, "All projects suffer from one, and only one, problem. It's known as *the big problem at the end.*" This is so true. All projects start with a wave of energy and euphoria, and, especially these days with the ubiquity of tools such as PC-based project planning software, complete with umpteen pages of bar charts, dependency diagrams, and task lists. And, sometime just before the end, so many projects are in a state of rancor, with prospective users feeling let down, financial managers wondering where the money went, and project managers feeling like they might have had a quieter life had they chosen to become professional heavyweight boxers.

This isn't a text on project management, but a few guidelines might be helpful.

Projects are intrinsically uncertain, and cannot be predicted with precision, in terms of both cost and elapsed time. Never produce (if you're a project manager) or believe (if you're on a steering committee) any plans that state "the project will be delivered by this date for this cost." Rather, identify and scrutinize the range of times for delivery and the range of likely costs. One of the key roles of the project manager is, of course, to identify all the tasks that need to be carried out, their mutual dependencies, and their resource requirements. This is the basis of the project plan, and the resource estimate. But an even more important role is for the project manager to identify all the uncertainties and risks that will cause the project to take longer than the "earliest" time estimate and the "lowest" cost, and to devise strategies for their identification and management. As a result, the project manager can then estimate the "latest" time and the "highest" cost. The project steering committee needs to review the analysis of the project uncertainty for wisdom, and help the project manager's risk assessment. If the project is in familiar territory, and there is much relevant collective experience, then the range of uncertainty should be small; if, on the other hand, the project is truly new, the range might be very broad – that's the way these things really are. The project might, in fact, cost the projected maximum, and if this is far too much for the organization to bear, then maybe it shouldn't embark on the project in the first place. For if the project is started, and begins to move along the expensive trajectory, you should not be too surprised as the optimistic estimates are dashed. And if the organization decides it can't afford it, then the project should be canceled – without destroying the career of the project manager, and all the members of the project team.

Hard-nosed managers – those who manage everything on time and within budget – are probably having apoplexy by now: how on earth can you condone, let alone advise, managing projects on the basis of ranges rather than deadlines? As soon as a range is mentioned, surely the project will immediately slip as the team slacks off?

I understand that, and that's why managing projects is a little more subtle. To keep the team focused and motivated, the project itself needs to be managed, on a day-to-day basis, to the "earliest" deadline, and the "lowest" cost: that way, everyone on the team is clear on what they have to do. The project steering committee, however, needs to be briefed on the possibility that the plans might need to be stretched, and one of their key roles is to release predetermined contingencies when necessary. The project manager needs to look in two directions at once, motivating the team to follow the "earliest" schedule, but keeping an eagle eye open for the signs of the necessity to go to the steering committee to recommend an extension. Pity the poor project manager, doomed to live in a permanent state of schizophrenia – striving to demonstrate leadership to the team to maximize the likelihood that the project can be delivered without the need for releasing contingencies; needing to be ever vigilant on assessing the risks; seeking not to appear to be "weak"; endeavoring to maintain the trust and respect of the steering committee, so that if in fact a recommendation to release contingency funds has to be made, the committee will do so, professionally and without blame. Not an easy role to play. No wonder some of the best people choose to stay within the safety and certainty of the line.

And the pressure increases as the project approaches completion. One of the most difficult decisions to take at the end of a project is to identify that it is indeed the end. In developing a system, there is always "one more bug"; in launching a new product, there is always a feature to tweak. When, precisely, is the system well-enough developed to be relied upon? When, precisely, is the product good enough to launch? To those who love tinkering, nothing is ever good enough; to those who are desperate for action, why oh why are we wasting all this time? The decision to cut over from "development" to "live" is critical – if this happens prematurely, the damage to the business might be irrecoverable; if too late, time and money might be being consumed needlessly. Wise organizations understand this, and develop, well in advance of the time for the "go-live" decision, a set of specific acceptance criteria.

ACCEPTANCE CRITERIA

Judging the end of a project is never a clean decision – nothing is ever perfect. The essence of the decision is to balance the business benefit of the launch (as represented by, for example, the sales of the new product, or the cost-savings of a new system) against the possibility of major failure. As ever, it is a question of risk.

A powerful way of managing the risk is by compiling, well in advance of the time the decision has to be made, a comprehensive list of "acceptance criteria." This is a comprehensive list not only of all the features of the new system (or whatever), but also of the associated performance characteristics. Suppose, for example, that the project is the building of a new call center. The list of features will be very long (certainly hundreds, and maybe thousands, of items), including all the features of the building, the systems infrastructure, training, and a myriad of other things too. Within that list will be a feature such as "Response time on incoming calls," and the performance characteristic might be "96% of all calls received on any day to be answered within three rings, a further 3% within four rings, and no calls at all after five rings"; the feature "Recruitment plans in place" might have the performance characteristic "The recruitment plan required to support months three to six of live operation has been defined, and signed off by the main board."

As the project nears completion, some form of test can take place at which all of these features can be measured, from which it is possible to determine which features have met the required performance levels, and which have not. This provides the steering committee with good, comprehensive information, on the basis of which they can assess the risk of "throwing the switch" even if some features are not quite right. If the risk is assessed as unacceptable, further development work can be authorized; if the risk is acceptable, then implementation can proceed, even in the light of known teething problems.

This method really works, and I have used it on many occasions: notably for the opening of a new office for Goldman Sachs in Paris (a project carried out to very tight deadlines), and also in relation to the "go live" decision for the TALISMAN project at the London Stock Exchange, which, at the time, was one of the largest projects in the UK, representing more than 1000 person-years of effort.

One last word on projects: they do come to an end. Some organizations seem to forget this, and once a project team has been created, it continues, seemingly for ever (like some committees you might have come across!). Wise organizations don't fall into this trap. They know that projects are finite; they anticipate their natural end; they ensure that all the team members are fully and successfully reintegrated into the line subsequently; and – most importantly – they capture the learning from the project, so that they do not make all the same mistakes again.

MANAGING THE PIPELINE OF IDEAS

As you will by now appreciate, there is a lot to be done in organizing all the activities required for building and maintaining an unlearning organization. Some of these things are in the natural domain of the line – changes to the budgeting process, for example, are legitimately best carried out by the finance department, and changes to the reward and remuneration system by HR.

It may be, however, that your organization does not have a process for managing innovation itself – especially managing the pipeline of ideas, from idea generation right across the Innovation Target to implementation. In that case, one needs to be built. This, as usual, will require a champion, probably someone at board level, and naturally (but not necessarily) the individual with prime responsibility for the processes for business and strategic planning. It will also require a manager (probably full time), and a modest infrastructure.

The primary role of this new function is to manage the pipeline of ideas. This entails:

» ensuring the individuals throughout the organization are equipped to participate in idea generation and evaluation;
» acting as a central focal point where all ideas are logged;
» administering the information system that captures all the ideas, and monitors their progress from one stage to the next across the Innovation Target;
» reviewing, from time to time, the ideas "on the shelf" to determine if any should be revisited, given current or expected future circumstances;
» acting as a central hub for information on creativity and innovation, providing support across the organization.

The role, as I have described it, is one of facilitation and networking: the role does not take responsibility for training, for example, but it is involved in making sure that training happens. The role therefore acts as a central coordinating hub, supporting the activities of the business units, and adding value by providing functions that the business units themselves cannot perform, such as acting as a central repository of all ideas, administering the system that tracks ideas as they move through the various stages of the Innovation Target, and – most importantly – providing a mechanism whereby ideas which have been shelved or rejected during the evaluation process (see page 21) are not totally lost, but can be reviewed from time to time in case something has changed. Over time, the organizational repository of ideas can be immensely valuable.

What this role is *not* is the "central innovation department" – this being the part of the organization whose job it is "to have ideas." In my view, such a department is the antithesis of the unlearning organization, for it institutionalizes the excuse "having ideas is nothing to do with my job – that's what that central department is for." In an unlearning organization, creativity and innovation are everyone's opportunity, and the role of the central department is to support this, to champion it, and to provide the infrastructure to help make it all work.

Summary

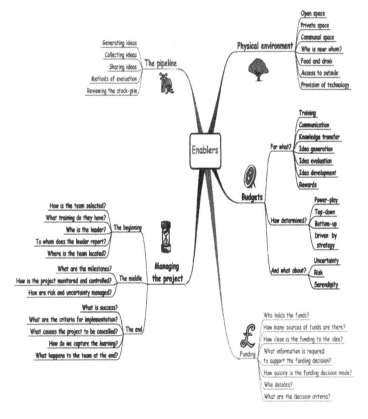

Fig. 7.3

Key Concepts and Thinkers

This chapter is a glossary of terms from **black hat** (a metaphor for one of the key roles required in balanced evaluation) to **yellow hat** (a metaphor for another of the key roles required in balanced evaluation).

Cross-references are indicated by the use of *bold italic*. Numbers in brackets refer to page references in the main text.

Black hat (38) - Metaphor for one of the roles to be played in the process of balanced and wise *evaluation* - the role that asks the question "What issues need to be managed to bring the idea to success?" This role is critical in understanding, and managing, the risks inevitably associated with *innovation*. See also *blue hat*, *green hat*, *purple hat*, *red hat*, *white hat*, and *yellow hat*.

Blockbuster (20) - An idea which, once implemented, achieves great success. Blockbusters are not necessarily *radical*.

Blue hat (45) - Metaphor for one of the roles to be played in the process of balanced and wise *evaluation* - the role that orchestrates the overall process. See also *black hat*, *green hat*, *purple hat*, *red hat*, *white hat*, and *yellow hat*.

Brain bank connectivity (*BBC*) (31) - The creativity-enhancing effect attributable to the connectedness between individuals.

Brainstorming - Idea generation technique that starts with a blank sheet of paper, and allows for free thinking in a safe environment. In my view, the use of the blank sheet of paper, which is a symbol of being unconstrained, is in fact counterproductive. *Innovation* in business never takes place on a greenfield site: rather, it takes place in the context of much learning, knowledge, experience, and success. The sheet of paper is not blank; it is very full indeed. Hence the power of *InnovAction!*

Business concept innovation - A concept advocated by Gary Hamel in his book *Leading the Revolution*, in which an organization's entire business model and strategy is radically changed.

Christiansen, James A. (56) - Author of *Competitive Innovation Management: Techniques to improve innovation performance* and *Building the Innovative Organization: Management systems that encourage innovation*, two books, both published in 2000, which describe the key cultural features of innovative organizations.

Creativity (4) - The capability to discover new ideas. There is a widely held belief that creativity is an innate gift, with which the fortunate few are born, while the rest of us wallow in an uncreative swamp. I do not believe this. In my view, creativity is a skill that can be learned, practiced, and enhanced. And as with all human abilities, some people will enjoy doing it more than others, some people will wish to spend more time doing it than others, and some people will be more effective at it than others. But it is an activity in which we can all contribute, and from which no one is excluded. Creativity is not the same thing as *innovation*: creativity is about generating new ideas; innovation is about generating new ideas **and** making something happen as a result.

Culture (3) - Organizational cultures have an enormous impact on whether or not it is "safe" to generate new ideas, and how any ideas are evaluated, developed, and implemented.

de Bono, Edward - Undoubtedly one of the leading thinkers, and certainly the most powerful evangelist, in the field of *creativity* and *innovation*. He is the originator of *lateral thinking*, and the author of a host of books, the best of which (to my mind) is *Serious Creativity*.

de Gues, Arie - A life-long employee of Royal-Dutch Shell who shot to fame with his book *The Living Organization* which draws a parallel between organizations and living beings. This is an important cultural concept, and has much relevance as regards fostering an innovative culture.

Evaluation (7) - The process by which ideas are judged as "good" or "bad," with the "bad" ones being rejected, and the "good" ones accepted from further exploration, development, and implementation. Evaluation is very important as regards the overall management of the entire *innovation* process (see *Innovation Target*), for it acts as a filter; it is also significant culturally. See also *premature evaluation* and *black hat*, *blue hat*, *green hat*, *purple hat*, *red hat*, *white hat*, and *yellow hat*.

Green hat (44) - Metaphor for one of the roles to be played in the process of balanced and wise *evaluation* the role that asks the question "What solutions can we identify to the problems identified by the black, red, and white hats?" See also *black hat*, *blue hat*, *purple hat*, *red hat*, *white hat*, and *yellow hat*.

Gundling, Ernest - Author of *The 3M Way to Innovation*, published in 2000, which is the first book since 1955 to present an in-depth insight into 3M, the company that many would regard as *the* role model for an innovative organization.

Hamel, Gary – Leading business guru, with a highly original and provocative style, who passionately believes in the power, and strategic importance, of *innovation*, as expressed in his latest book *Leading the Revolution*, published in 2000.

How might this be different? (5) – The central question in the *InnovAction!* process, which takes a feature of the *focus of attention* as we know it today, and encourages you to explore how that might be different, so facilitating *unlearning* and creating the conditions for the discovery of new ideas.

Idea generation (2) – The central process of *innovation*, in which new ideas are created deliberately and systematically. Since innovation in business never occurs on a greenfield site, the key skill required is that of *unlearning*. All the tools and techniques to support creativity and idea generation are vehicles to help you unlearn, and they largely fall into two categories: *springboards* and *retro-fits*. See also *Innovation Target* and *InnovAction!*

Implementation (2) – The final stage of *innovation*, in which an idea comes to full fruition. See also *Innovation Target*.

Incremental ideas (20) – Ideas whose features are only modestly changed, as compared to their antecedents or predecessors. Many incremental ideas have turned out to be *blockbusters*. See also *radical ideas*.

InnovAction! (5) – A powerful technique for *idea generation* that takes as its starting point a list of features of the *focus of attention* as it exists now. By asking *"How might this be different?"* you are actively encouraged to discover new ideas. Unlike *brainstorming*, which starts from a blank sheet of paper, and *lateral thinking*, which seems to conjure *provocative operations* out of thin air, *InnovAction!* recognizes that the *focus of attention* is likely to be associated with considerable learning, knowledge, and experience, which *InnovAction!* actively uses as a *springboard* to new ideas.

Innovation (2) – The active management of the four-stage process of *idea generation*, *evaluation*, *development*, and *implementation*, as applied to the domains of *new product development*, *process innovation*, *organizational innovation*, *relationship innovation*, *strategy*, and *you*.

Innovation Target (3) - A diagrammatic representation of the four stages of *innovation* (*idea generation, evaluation, development,* and *implementation*) as an archery target, on which are superposed the six domains where innovation can take place (*new product development, process innovation, organizational innovation, relationship innovation, strategy,* and *you*).

Innovative organizations (56) - Organizations which have created, built, and sustained an internal capability to make *innovation*, in all its richness, an integral part of their operations. Such organizations are able to solve problems, grasp opportunities, and create their own futures again and again and again and again.

Koestler, Arthur - Scholar, soldier, and author of many books, including *The Act of Creation*, in which is to be found *Koestler's Law*.

Koestler's Law (4) - To my mind, the most powerful definition of creativity: the creative act is not an act of creation in the sense of the Old Testament. It does not create something out of nothing; it uncovers, selects, re-shuffles, combines, synthesizes already existing facts, ideas, faculties, skills. The more familiar the parts, the more striking the new whole.

Landscape metaphor for learning - A metaphor which compares the internal structure of our brains to a richly carved landscape of mountains and valleys. The process of learning is portrayed as the creation of the valleys by the action of rain and rivers, so that, once we have learnt something, we are swept down the appropriate valley, and can execute the appropriate actions and behaviors with ease for example, getting dressed, crossing the road, or driving a car. These activities, of course, are not contentious; but the same applies to more sophisticated activities, such as managing staff, or formulating strategy, too. Within this metaphor, *innovation* is a process of escaping from the valley of familiarity, in which a "raindrop" is scooped out of the bottom of a valley, placed on a neighboring ridge, and allowed to remain in this unstable state until it falls into a new valley, the valley of innovation.

Lateral thinking - A technique of *idea generation* developed by *Edward de Bono*, based on the concept of the "*provocative operation*," which de Bono calls "po." A provocative operation is a deliberate shock to the way we usually see things, and is used as a mechanism to jolt our thinking into new ideas. Two well-known examples of this are "po:planes fly upside down" and "po:a factory is upstream of itself."

Learning – A process in which experience becomes consolidated so that certain behaviors can be repeated, or knowledge recalled, at will. It is now well established that during learning, *neurons* in our brains become "hard-wired," thereby creating semi-permanent neural circuits that store memories, or control learned behaviors. Frequent recall of the memory, or repetition of an action, strengthens these circuits; lack of use allows them to break down, this being an explanation of forgetting. See also *landscape metaphor for learning* and *Donald Hebb*.

Learning organization – An organization which has institutionalized a spirit of learning.

Neuron – A cell in the nervous system. *Learning* is a process in which semi-permanent connections are made among specific neurons, so forming a neural circuit which can be activated at will to recall a memory or repeat a learned behavior.

New product development (2) – One of the domains where *innovation* is important. See *Innovation Target*.

Organizational innovation (2) – One of the domains where *innovation* is important. See *Innovation Target*.

Premature evaluation (12) – A condition, often exhibited by aggressive males, who, in a fit of over-excitement, evaluate ideas far too soon, thereby killing *innovation* stone dead, and creating a most unsatisfying situation for everybody!

Process innovation (2) – One of the domains where *innovation* is important, and sometimes portrayed as business process reengineering. See *Innovation Target*.

Product innovation (2) – One of the domains where *innovation* is important. See *Innovation Target*.

Purple hat (45) – Metaphor for one of the roles to be played in the process of balanced and wise *evaluation*; the role that asks the question "What actions should we take in the light of our analysis so far?" This role is critical in taking decisions as to implementing the idea, shelving the idea, or committing further resources for further analysis. See also *black hat, blue hat, green hat, red hat, white hat*, and *yellow hat*.

Radical ideas (20) – Ideas whose features are significantly different from its antecedents or predecessors. Many people believe that only radical ideas can be *blockbusters*, but this is rarely the case; many radical ideas are just too different to be well accepted. See also *incremental ideas*.

Raindrop in the valley metaphor for learning – See *landscape metaphor for learning*.

Red hat (40) – Metaphor for one of the roles to be played in the process of balanced and wise *evaluation* the role that asks the question "What constituencies (groups of people and individuals) will be affected by the idea, both when it is implemented, and also during implementation?" This role is critical in understanding, and managing, the different personal reactions likely to be associated with the implementation of a new idea. See also *black hat, blue hat, green hat, purple hat, white hat*, and *yellow hat*.

Relationship innovation (2) – One of the domains where *innovation* is important, applying to the development of new forms of relationship, both within an organization and across the organization's external boundaries. See *Innovation Target*.

Retro-fits (4) – A set of techniques for *idea generation* in which your mind is deliberately projected to a place very distant from the chosen *focus of attention*. From this distant standpoint, you are then encouraged to try to discover some connections back to the *focus of attention*, so discovering new ideas. Examples of retro-fit techniques are *analogy, metaphor, random word*, and *simile*.

Senge, Peter – Author of the business bestseller *The Fifth Discipline*, and advocate of systems thinking and the *learning organization*.

Silver bullet (116) – Something specific that brings enormous value to your business, such as a *blockbuster* product, a unique business process, or a global brand.

Silver bullet machine (116) – The organizational capability to produce *silver bullets* again and again and again, so conferring on the organization the ultimate competitive advantage.

Six Thinking Hats (34) – A technique established by *Edward de Bono*, and positioned by him as a technique for *idea generation*.

My personal view is that the technique is much more powerful as one of *evaluation*. See also *black hat*, *blue hat*, *green hat*, *purple hat*, *red hat*, *white hat*, and *yellow hat*.

Springboards (4) – A set of techniques for *idea generation* which take as the starting point the knowledge, learning, and experience you have of the *focus of attention* as it is now. This detailed information is then used as a springboard for generating new ideas by asking the question *How might this be different?* The main technique here is my own *InnovAction!*

Strategy innovation (2) – One of the domains where *innovation* is important, applying to the development of new business strategies. See *Innovation Target*.

Unlearning (4) – The process by which your knowledge, learning, and experience of a chosen *focus of attention* is decomposed into its component parts. This is a necessary part of the creative process, for this then releases the basic components which can then be reformed into new patterns in accordance with *Koestler's Law*. Most people find this very difficult not least because much of our success is attributable to our knowledge, learning, and experience, and the process of disaggregating, decomposing, and challenging these is often most uncomfortable. It is, however, the key to creativity. Unlearning must never be portrayed as an attack on the past, or as critical, blaming, or destructive: rather, it is a constructive process which is a necessary step toward building an innovative future.

Unlearning organization (62) – An organization which has institutionalized the processes of *unlearning*, and in which unlearning is not regarded as a threat. Such organizations therefore have built a fundamental capability for discovering new ideas, and so are in a position to capture ultimate competitive advantage.

White hat (42) – Metaphor for one of the roles to be played in the process of balanced and wise *evaluation* the role that asks the question "What data do we need to take an informed decision?" This role is critical as regards ensuring that there is a robust foundation of relevant facts on which a decision can be based. See also *black hat*, *blue hat*, *green hat*, *purple hat*, *red hat*, and *yellow hat*.

Yellow hat (36) – Metaphor for one of the roles to be played in the process of balanced and wise *evaluation* the role that asks the question "What benefits will arise as a result of successfully implementing the idea?" This role is critical as regards gaining a deep understanding of the benefits associated with the idea. See also *black hat*, *blue hat*, *green hat*, *purple hat*, *red hat*, and *white hat*.

Resources

This chapter refers you to 16 key books and 10 useful Websites.

There is a lot of good material on innovation, and here is my personal choice.

BOOKS

» *?What if! How to start a creative revolution at work*, by Dave Allan, Matt Kingdon, Kris Murrin, and Daz Rudkin, published by Capstone, Oxford, 1999

A lively discussion of "?What if!"'s view on innovation: I particularly enjoyed the chapter on making ideas real.

» *The Innovator's Dilemma – When new technologies cause great firms to fail*, by Clayton M. Christensen, published by Harvard Business School Press, Boston, Massachusetts, 1997

Winner of the Financial Times – Booz.Allen and Hamilton "Best Business book of 1997" award, this book lucidly tells how organizations can do many things right, but still end up failing: total customer focus, for example (a "good thing"), can blind a company to things customers aren't asking for, or to look for new markets. What these companies fail to do is to manage what Christensen calls "disruptive innovation," and his book tells you how to avoid falling into this trap.

» *Competitive Innovation Management: Techniques to improve innovation performance*, by James A. Christensen, published by Macmillan Business, Basingstoke, 2000

» *Building the Innovative Organization: Management systems that encourage innovation*, by James A. Christensen, published by Macmillan Business, Basingstoke, 2000

These two books are a matching pair, being based on Chrisensen's PhD thesis at INSEAD which studied twenty organizations, eight in depth (including 3M and Eastman Chemical), to discover what made some organizations highly innovative, and others less so. Very thorough, and highly informative.

» *Serious Creativity*, by Edward de Bono, published by HarperCollins, London, 1993

A compendium of de Bono's work over the past 25 years.

» *Six Action Shoes*, by Edward de Bono, published by HarperCollins, London, 1991

In which de Bono uses the metaphor of differently colored shoes and boots to depict six different action styles.

» *Six Thinking Hats*, by Edward de Bono, published by Viking, London, 1986

An exposition of de Bono's process for evaluating ideas safely, using the metaphor of wearing colored hats to legitimize the key roles.

» *The Living Company: Growth, learning and longevity in business*, by Arie de Geus, published by Nicholas Brealey Publishing, London, 1997

A powerful rallying call to those who believe in the importance of the human spirit in organizations – even large ones. The central metaphor is the organization as a living being.

» *The 3M Way to Innovation: Balancing people and profit*, by Ernest Gundling, published by Kodansha International, New York, 2000

3M is widely regarded as *the* role model of the innovative organization, and although 3M is widely reported in case studies, this is the first full-length book on 3M to be published since 1955.

» *Scenarios: The art of strategic conversation*, by Kees van der Heijden, published by John Wiley & Sons, Chichester, 1997

A well-written discussion of scenario planning by a leading member of the Shell scenario planning community.

» *The Age of Innovation: Making business creativity a competence, not a coincidence*, by Felix Janszen, published by Financial Times Prentice Hall, London, 2000

A rather different approach to how to build a culture of innovation, embracing the principles of systems thinking and system dynamics modeling.

» *Radical Innovation: How mature companies can outsmart upstarts*, by Richard Leifer and Christopher M. McDermott, published by Harvard Business School Press, Boston, Massachusetts, 2001

This book covers similar territory to Christensen, being based on fieldwork at companies such as General Motors, General Electric, du Pont and IBM.

» *Scenario Planning: Managing for the future*, by Gill Ringland, published by John Wiley & Sons, Chichester, 1998

A comprehensive description of most of the different methods of scenario planning.

» *Serious Play: How the world's best companies simulate to innovate*, by Michael Schrage, published by Harvard Business School Press, Boston Massachusetts, 2000

This book stresses the importance of making new ideas as real as possible.

» *Smart Things to Know about Innovation and Creativity*, by Dennis Sherwood, published by Capstone, Oxford, 2001

My most recent book on innovation, packed with examples and case studies, and with a full explanation not only of *InnovAction!*, but of the cultural requirements for building a truly innovative organization too.

» *Unlock Your Mind: A guide to deliberate and systematic innovation*, by Dennis Sherwood, published by Gower Publishing, Basingstoke, 1998

My early book on innovation, with quite a lot on systems thinking too.

WEBSITES

If you type "innovation" or "creativity" into a search engine, don't be surprised if you get literally hundreds of thousands of hits. Here are just a very few of them:

» www.buffalostate.edu/~creatcnt

The home page of the Centre for Studies in Creativity, the research institute set up by Alex Osborne, the inventor of brainstorming. www.buffalostate.edu/~creatcnt/links.html is the address of their links page, which is both comprehensive and independent.

» www.businessinnovation.ey.com

The home page for the Centre for Business Innovation of consultants Ernst & Young (now part of the CAP-Gemini empire).

» www.cordis.lu/innovation/

The home page of the European Commission's INNOVATION program.

» www.cul.co.uk

The home page of Creativity Unleashed Limited.

» www.edwdebono.com

Edward de Bono's official Website.

» www.expertson.com/Innovation/innovation

   A US site covering all aspects of innovation, with many links.

» www.mckinsey.com

   The home page of the most prestigious consulting firm, McKinsey & Co. Their journal, *The McKinsey Quarterly*, is always worth browsing.

» www.silverbulletmachine.com

   My own Website!

» www.strategos.com

   The home page of Gary Hamel's consulting firm, Strategos.

» www.thinksmart.com

   The home page of the Innovation Network, who, among many other things, offer an Innovation University.

So, What Can You Actually Do?

This chapter gives you pragmatic guidance on what you can actually do to make your organizational culture more innovative.

This title has been about organizational culture – the way the organization actually behaves, the unwritten but oh-so-powerful rules of
behavior, the reality of how people are encouraged and rewarded, and
discouraged and penalized. Yes, cultures can be changed, but it can
be a long, slow process, especially if you believe in the (somewhat
gloomy, but nonetheless realistic) message of the next box.

DO ORGANIZATIONS END UP WITH THE CULTURES THEY DESERVE?

Organizational cultures are created, and perpetuated, by
people – there is no other way for cultures to happen. Today's
leaders appoint their successors, and, if they don't exactly select
people who remind them of themselves, they are most likely to
select those whose behaviors comply.

What of those individuals whose behaviors don't comply? They
have but three choices. They can willingly change their own
behaviors to come into line, and many people do that. Secondly,
they can reach the same endpoint but grudgingly, without causing
too much fuss, but enough fuss when the time is right. And a lot
of people do that too. And the third choice is to leave, in the hope
that the next organization will have behavioral norms that align
more naturally with their own.

Over time, does the population that remains within the organization necessarily become more culturally homogeneous, in essence
of their own volition?

Do organizations therefore end up with the cultures they
deserve?

So how do you change something as amorphous as the corporate
culture? How do you relax a tendency to avoid risks without betting
the company? How do you encourage people to move out of the safety
of the line, and be willing to cope with uncertainties of an innovation
project? How do you break down the silos and the power bases, and
encourage a richer spirit of sharing and teamwork?

My personal experience is that to try to change "the culture" is too
big an undertaking: success is far more likely if you set out to change

a series of specific processes, a step at a time, within a consistent overall framework. This is totally consistent with the message given on page 57: to become an innovative organization, to build an unlearning organization, you need to have two big things – the will to do it, and some financial headroom – and then lots and lots of little things need to be consistent and harmonious.

If the two big things are there, then, rather than tackling "the culture" as a whole, do a series of consistent projects to change those specific little things that will help – maybe it's the budgeting system to allow for innovation projects, maybe training, maybe the criteria for promotion. As these progressively and consistently become aligned, the culture – which is manifest by how many of these things work in practice – will shift too.

But where do you start? The checklist of little things (as an *aide-mémoire*, see the mind maps on pages 84 and 95) is enormously long; the task, surely, is daunting. Well, it might be, but I'd be truly surprised. In my experience, is it remarkably rare for *everything* on the checklist to be totally counter-productive or dysfunctional: usually, some things are in good shape; some things are neutral; some things are a problem, but not hugely so; and some things require fixing.

So the starting point is the checklist. Use the checklist to scout round your organization, and do a quick diagnostic. For each of the items on the checklist, ask:

» How does this work now?
» Does this encourage innovation actively, is it neutral, or is it a positive disincentive?
» If it is neutral or negative, how might it be different? (Aha! ***InnovAction!*** strikes again!).

This enables you to segregate the host of little things into three categories – those that are fine, those that aren't fine but aren't causing pain, and those that are causing pain, and need to be fixed. When this is done, you can then define a series of well-focused, manageable, finite projects, with targeted deliverables, and a much higher chance of success. Some of them may be big and difficult – like changing the reward structure – but even if it is big and difficult (as indeed it is), it is still, with energy, appropriate resourcing, and the right political support (the first being what you provide, and the other two being consequences of the two "big things"), manageable and doable. And you can do it, and it will succeed. And once that has happened, you can move on to the next project, and then the next, so that, over a sensible period of time, a series of projects have been successfully delivered, all of which have nudged those little things into alignment, so changing the culture, and resulting in your contributing to building a truly innovative culture, a real unlearning organization.

And you'll have built something else too. You will have built your organization's own silver bullet machine, so you can manufacture those oh-so-valuable magic silver bullets again and again and again and again. That, surely, must be the ultimate competitive advantage.

TWELVE KEY FEATURES OF THE UNLEARNING ORGANIZATION

1 **The day-job doesn't get in the way.** Unlearning organizations make time for thinking, exploration, innovation. They don't let the pressures of the day-job stop this.

2 **"If it ain't broke, don't fix it" is *not* "the way we do things around here."** Unlearning organizations don't wait for things to break before they fix them. They are always searching for better ways of doing things, even if there is no explicit "problem" to solve.

3 **The only rule is "rules are for breaking."** Unlearning organizations recognize that rules, policies, procedures, processes, are artifacts of the time they were originated. All are constantly under review, and those that remain fit-for-purpose are retained, those that have passed their sell-by date are ditched.

4 **Negligence is distinguished from learning.** Unlearning organizations know that "failure" is a very broad term, and embraces many things. In particular, they distinguish between "negligence" (the deliberate departure from an agreed policy) and "learning" (what happens when an outcome differs from

expectations). They do not condone the former; nor do they penalize the latter.

5 **They listen.** To each other, to the outside world. Actively. Bosses do not finish the sentences of their subordinates; peers use their ears more than their mouths.

6 **They share.** Resources, information, people, risk. They operate in highly connected networks rather than hierarchical silos; nothing is "mine," for everything is "ours"; everyone is comfortable playing whatever roles are fit-for-purpose at the time.

7 **They say "yes" more than they say "no."** Go to a meeting. Take a blank sheet of paper, draw a vertical line down the middle. Label the left-hand column "yes," the right-hand column "no." Each time you hear the word "yes," or an equivalent positive remark, place a tick in the left-hand column; likewise for "no" and its surrogates. In an unlearning organization, you will have far more ticks on the left than the right.

8 **They don't rush to judge.** Unlearning organizations know when to evaluate ideas, and do this only when there is a full and well-balanced view. They do not shoot from the hip, or jerk from the knee: they think from the head.

9 **They have a wise approach to managing risk.** Unlearning organizations fully recognize that innovation is all about managing risk. They also know full well that, in today's business climate – and especially tomorrow's – to maintain the status quo, though comfortable and familiar, is likely to be more risky than stepping wisely into the unknown. They do not expect every innovation to succeed, nor do they place any foolhardy bets.

10 **Their performance measures support innovation, rather than discourage it.** Unlearning organizations have enhanced their portfolio of performance measures to ensure that they support, rather than inhibit, innovation. Even to the (unusual) extent of measuring inputs (such as hours spent on idea generation) rather than outputs (number of ideas put into the suggestion box).

11 **They are very good at managing both the line *and* projects**

> "Did you hear about Pat?"
> "No, I don't think so. What's going on?"
> "He's been assigned to a "special" project."
> "Well, he's on his way out then."

That is a conversation you will not hear in an unlearning organization. Managing the line and managing projects exist easily side by side; being assigned to an innovation project is a symbol of regard; and risk-taking is rewarded.

12 **They regard innovation as a core business process in its own right**. Unlearning organizations manage innovation, in all its aspects, as a core business process, indeed as *the* core business process, forming the very heart of the organization's silver bullet machine. For they know that innovation – the ability to solve problems wherever they might arise, to be able to grasp opportunities however fleeting, to be confident in generating stunning new ideas again and again and again and again, and to deliver them too – is truly *the* ultimate competitive advantage.

Frequently Asked Questions (FAQs)

Q1: What's the difference between creativity and innovation?

A: See Chapter 1, Introduction.

Q2: My organization has no problem in coming up with great ideas – we have pages of flip-charts full of them. Our problem is the next step – from this huge number of ideas of all different shapes and sizes, how can we distinguish the "good" ones from the "bad" ones, so that we invest in the right places?

A: See Chapter 3, Section: Evaluation as a business process.

Q3: I've heard about those funny colored hats – but what exactly is this all about?

A: See Chapter 6.

Q4: My boss says that the only really good ideas – those that are the real blockbusters – have to be radical. Is he right?

A: See Chapter 3, Section: The evaluation sieve and the evaluation grid.

Q5: My organization isn't very innovative right now, and I want it to become more so. We must be missing some "magic ingredient." What is it?

A: See Chapter 7, Section: What distinguishes an innovative organization from an uninnovative one?

Q6: How much should I allow in my budget for innovation?

A: See Chapter 7, Section: What are the two big things? and Chapter 7, Section: Budgets.

Q7: How do I design an incentive system that really encourages my team to be more innovative, and rewards them accordingly?

A: See Chapter 7, Section: Reward and recognition.

Q8: My company has just spent a fortune sending everyone on a one-day training program in creativity. The course was great – but, in practice, nothing has changed. That money not only went down the drain, but my team are somehow more restless now than they were before! What went wrong?

A: See Chapter 7, Section: Training.

Q9: We already have a keen emphasis on quality, and have introduced best practice processes such as Total Quality Management and Lean Manufacturing. The emphasis here is very much on finding new ways of solving problems, and we're already good at that. Isn't this innovation in practice? What else is there?

A: See Chapter 7, Section: Embedding innovation into the day-job.

Q10: I've heard the term scenario planning – but what exactly is it?

A: See Chapter 7, Section: Innovation and scenario planning.

Q11: Where can I find a good checklist we can use to help our organization to become more innovative?

A: See Chapter 7, Section: Culture is all about practice, Chapter 7, Section: Scenario planning, and Chapter 7, Section: Managing projects.

About the Author

Dennis Sherwood originally trained as a research scientist, and was for twelve years an IT consulting partner with Deloitte, Haskins + Sells, and, following the merger in the UK, Coopers & Lybrand. He was then appointed an Executive Director with Goldman Sachs in London, and is now the Managing Director of The Silver Bullet Machine Manufacturing Company Limited, which specializes in organizational creativity and innovation. Dennis is well known on the conference circuit, and is the author of five books, including *Smart Things to Know about Innovation and Creativity*, published by Capstone in 2001.

Index

Printed and bound by CPI Group (UK) Ltd, Croydon, CR0 4YY

13/04/2025

14656565-0004